The BRIGHTON & SUSSEX Cook Book

A celebration of the amazing food & drink on our doorstep.

FOREWORD

Brighton has always been known to do its own thing. The food scene is no different to this and we pride ourselves on doing things that little bit differently, focussing on our local produce and supporting local suppliers.

When I decided that I wanted to open a restaurant, I knew it would be in Brighton, well Hove, actually. Not only do we have incredible food producers on our doorstep throughout Sussex, but there's something about everyone's willingness for you to succeed that makes it feel like home.

Brighton has an eclectic mix of fantastic restaurants, bars and cafes and I think there's something here for everyone. The people of Brighton are always open to trying something new which allows me and the team to push our boundaries, knowing that people will try something and give us their honest feedback.

Looking out to the sea from one window and onto the rolling South Downs from another is a real luxury. Sussex is home to burgeoning vineyards, artisan cheesemakers and organic butchers – there's nowhere better.

Sussex boasts a landscape of rolling countryside dotted with medieval villages, where history is alive and well in the cobbled streets. The stunning coastline attracts visitors from all over the country and provides mouth-watering fresh fish for the local restaurants.

At the heart of Sussex, Brighton's food offer is broad. It's a very special city that has been very kind to us. Maybe it's that sea air… or maybe it's being part of the wonderful county of Sussex with its incredible bounty of produce.

Steven Edwards

CONTENTS

The Brighton & Sussex Cook Book

©2017 Meze Publishing. All rights reserved.

First edition printed in 2017 in the UK.

ISBN: 978-1-910863-22-0

Thank you to: Steven Edwards, etch.

Compiled by: Jonathan Heath

Written by: Kate Reeves-Brown

*Photography by: Xavier Buendia
(www.xdbphotography.com)*

Additional photography: Frankie Knight

Edited by: Phil Turner

Designed by: Paul Cocker, Tom Crosby

PR: Kerre Chen, Sarah Gunton, Laura Wolvers

*Contributors: Faye Bailey, Katie Fisher,
Sarah Koriba, Anna Tebble*

Cover art: Luke Prest (www.lukeprest.com)

Published by Meze Publishing Limited

Unit 1b, 2 Kelham Square

Kelham Riverside

Sheffield S3 8SD

Web: www.mezepublishing.co.uk

Tel: 0114 275 7709

Email: info@mezepublishing.co.uk

Double-cooked
AND SAUCY

Inspired by the irresistible fries of Belgium,
BeFries has elevated the humble chip to new heights...

Brothers Dashal and Chan opened their unique eatery in August 2016 following years of planning. Dashal and his older sister Ezda were born in the Netherlands before moving back to the UK as children. In subsequent years, the whole family would often return to visit Amsterdam. On every single visit, the thing they would look forward to the most was a cone of Belgian fries – soft and fluffy on the inside, crisp on the outside and topped with an endless choice of sauces.

Chef Chan and record label owner Dashal decided to join forces and open the country's very first Belgian fries restaurant. After two years planning and researching, they imported a Belgian fryer and decided upon Agria potatoes, a variety developed by the Dutch and also used by the Belgians.

The chips are hand-cut to a specific size (8-14mm) and then double-cooked for that oh-so-irresistible texture. The first frying is at a low temperature and renders the inside of the chips fluffy and light. The chips are then dried and allowed to rest before being fried at a high temperature to order – this second frying creates that crispy and grease-free exterior.

Anyone who has eaten Belgian fries in Europe will know there is so much more to the perfect serving than the chips themselves – cue the multitude of sauces available. Dashal and Chan have gone for a selection that incorporates classics (such as Belgian mayo, Dutch mayo, curry ketchup and frites sauce) alongside some inspired ideas (think spicy vegan tofu sauce, jerk mayo, and dill and gherkin mayo). They are constantly developing new flavours for the specials board, too.

The pair have been helped by their brother Joe (who is a chef) and sister Ezda (who worked in retail and brought a wealth of customer service experience to the team), to create a truly independent family business. They are all passionate about the product and business, as are all of the staff, which might explain why they have found themselves in Brighton's top three restaurants on Trip Advisor after only a year of business.

This socially conscious business has become a firm favourite in Brighton. They feed the homeless community at the end of each day, pay the living wage to their valued team and work to create local partnerships within the community. As they embark on their second year of business, the whole BeFries family is excited about what else they can achieve.

BeFries
SMOKED CHILLI KETCHUP

Sweet, smokey and spicy, this is a truly delicious accompaniment to perfectly cooked Belgian fries. We usually make this in a much larger batch, but we have scaled it down to a more manageable size for the home kitchen.

Preparation time: 10 minutes | Cooking time: 30 minutes | Makes 400ml

Ingredients

100g onions

5g garlic

1 tsp olive oil

1 tsp smoked paprika

1 tsp salt

1 tsp white wine vinegar

200ml passata

60g chipotle in adobo sauce

100g ketchup

Method

Finely chop the onions and garlic. Heat the oil in a pan, add the onions and garlic, and gently fry on a low heat until softened.

Add the paprika, salt and vinegar to the onions and continue to cook on a low heat for a further 10 minutes.

Add the passata and chipotle sauce and allow to simmer for 10 minutes.

Remove from the heat, add the ketchup and stir. Season to taste.

Serve with a portion of freshly cooked chips!

How we make the
PERFECT FRY

From choosing the correct potato, cut to the optimum size and frying to perfection - there is far more to the ultimate Belgian fry than you might think.

Home Grown for Freshness

Our traditional process starts with selecting a special variety of potato that is sourced from British farmers, ensuring a fresh supply.

Cut to Perfection

Once the potatoes are peeled, we cut them to a thickness that is ideal for double-cooked Belgian Fries.

First Fry

We fry at a low temperature in a unique, rounded-base basketless fryer, which allows them to move freely and cook evenly.

Drain & Dry

We drain and dry the fries, removing excess moisture, ideal for a crispy final fry.

Second Fry

The fries go in for a final fry where the heat of the oil is higher, producing a soft and fluffy centre and a deliciously crispy crust.

Ready to Go

We salt the fries in our special shaker and serve them up in a cone with your choice of sauce, ready to enjoy anywhere.

Spreading HAPPINESS

Brighton favourite Bluebird Tea Co. is mixing things up in 2018 with a new face for their independent, award-winning tea mixology...

Transforming blue-sky thinking to blue-sky drinking, the quirky, independent Brighton-based Bluebird Tea Co. is a dynamic young business with creativity at its heart. They are intent on putting a smile into each and every day with their original tea blends.

Their name has become known around Brighton thanks to the way this small business grew within the city to become one of the country's leading tea innovators. From their roots as Bluebird, the mixologists are moving into 2018 with new branding that will continue to communicate the innovative, friendly and fun ethos of the company.

So where did the original name come from? Owners Krisi and Mike, who met at university and are now married, were inspired by the term 'bluebird day' when living in Canada. It denotes a perfect day with bright blue skies; the type of day where people smile and it feels like anything is possible.

On returning to the UK, they decided to make Brighton the home for their new venture. The vibrant city seemed to be the perfect place to launch their creative tea-blending business.

Brighton is fun, friendly, easy-going and creative – everything they wanted to achieve in their brand.

When they opened their first unit, Krisi and Mike worked every hour in the shop, followed by evenings packing online orders in the basement – not to mention the continual process of developing new tea blend ideas (something which, four years later, Krisi still does for every new blend).

Just one look at the shelves and it's clear that fun and flavour come first. These are teas to make you smile. Although they have now created over 100 types, they are still always creating new flavours inspired by the seasons. Think Strawberry Lemonade in summer (lovely served chilled) or Gingerbread Chai in the winter. Their teas can be ordered from the website – shipping to an impressive 65 countries!

Krisi and Mike crowd-sourced for funds to expand the business and they are now proud to have 280 shareholders, all of whom are customers and fans of their award-winning teas, which are all hand-blended in the south of England.

LEMONADE

When life gives you lemons, brew lemonade.

BLUE RASPBER

JASMINE POACHED PEARS

Jasmine green tea lightly scented with fruity pear

PURE GRADE MATCHA

ave a Bluebird Day...

Welcome to Bluebird Tea Co.!
We are the UK's expert Tea Mixologists on a
mission to spread happiness one cup at a time.

We are a local, independent business who,
in just a few short years, have grown from
packing tea in our bedroom to Brighton's
sunny south coast. We create all of our blend
recipes + hand pack them in our little
warehouse in Hove.

Th   es from the skiing term meaning
           with blue skies and fresh snow.
         hen everything is beautiful +
        sible. It is flying. It is freedom.

COLDBREW TEA
Fruit Salad

COLDBREW TEA
Fruit Salad

Pandalicious Liquorice

Bluebird Tea Co.
IT'S A PERFECT MATCHA GIN DROP

A tea twist on a classic cocktail, this sweet yet sharp lemon and honey gin drop
uses Japanese matcha tea powder – packed full of green goodness,
with a hint of bitterness.

Preparation time: 10 minutes | Serves 1

Ingredients

½ tsp matcha tea powder

100ml warm water

25ml good-quality gin (we
recommend Brighton Gin or Millers)

1 tsp good-quality honey

1 lemon

½ cup ice

Matcha powder and sugar, to
decorate the glass

Method

Put the matcha powder into a cocktail shaker, add the warm water and whisk well until dissolved. Add the gin and honey (warm it first in the microwave if solid). Cut the lemon in half and squeeze in the juice from one half, reserving the other half for the garnish. Add the ice and roll in the shaker to combine, but do not shake!

Use a slice of the reserved lemon half to rim the glass edge, then dip the rim onto a plate of matcha powder and sugar.

Pour the cocktail into the glass. Cut another slice of lemon from the reserved lemon half and peel a lemon twirl to garnish the glass.

Wine
AND DINE

The pretty Sussex countryside is home to one of the country's first commercial vineyards, The Bolney Wine Estate, whose award-winning English wine is putting Sussex on the world wine map.

Family-run vineyard, The Bolney Wine Estate, was established in 1972 by Rodney and Janet Pratt, and today the business is run by their daughter, Sam, who is the head winemaker. Rodney was inspired by a trip to Germany, where he was impressed by the extensive winemaking in a climate that was notably similar to the south of England.

When he and Janet founded their own vineyard in the Sussex countryside, The Bolney Wine Estate was one of only six commercial vineyards in the UK. This long-neglected art was about to have a resurgence in this country, and Rodney would become one of the 20th-century pioneers of English wine.

Of course, when they first set out, very little was known about winemaking in the region, and it is thanks to many years of experimentation and passion that The Bolney Wine Estate developed to become an award-winning producer. In 2017, they accumulated an impressive haul of seven gold medals.

Head winemaker Sam Linter praises the unique microclimate that surrounds their vineyard for the success they have had with growing in the area. Along with the sheltered location that protects the vines from the elements, it is also set on a gentle slope that allows for good drainage. The Bolney Wine Estate inhabits a special spot in the Sussex countryside.

Being close to Brighton, The Bolney Wine Estate has become a popular destination for day trips. As well as three different tours of the vineyards, masterclasses and a beautiful vineyard trail, there is also a lovely shop and café on the premises.

The café serves breakfast and lunch, with dishes being carefully crafted using local produce. Monmouth coffee and a range of teas are available, although many guests choose to pair their lunch with a glass of wine from The Bolney Wine Estate itself. The sunny terrace overlooking the vineyard is perhaps the perfect spot to sample the wine while enjoying a bite to eat.

Rodney's oldest grandchild Charlotte has now joined the family business, too, adding a third generation to the ranks. With the younger grandchildren following at her heels, The Bolney Wine Estate looks set for a strong future as a family business for many more years to come.

Bolney Wine Estate
PEAR & BLUE CHEESE SALAD

This is a classic combination of flavours
and it works brilliantly with Brighton Blue.

Preparation time: 15 minutes | Serves 1

Ingredients

50g mixed salad with rocket

50g pea shoots

Olive oil

Salt and pepper

30g red onion

50g Brighton Blue cheese

30g walnuts

½ pear

Honey and mustard dressing

Method

Wash the salad and pea shoots and dress in olive oil, salt and pepper. Thinly slice the onion with a fine knife or mandoline, and add to the leaves.

Cut the cheese into bite-size chunks or crumble over the top.

Crush half of the walnuts and leave the rest whole. Mix the walnuts into the salad leaves.

Thinly slice the pear and arrange on top. Drizzle the dressing over the salad for the finishing touch!

This is lovely served with a glass of The Bolney Estate Lychgate White. Named after the Bolney Church lychgate (which is a roofed gateway into the churchyard), this fruity, zesty blend of Reichensteiner, Schonburger and Wurzer grapes has rich, ripe scents and flavours of lychee and passion fruit, which are balanced by a crisp, spicy acidity and refreshing elderflower notes. Perfect with this delicious salad.

It's in the roast and THE BLEND

Coffee roasters, tea blenders, café and food/craft academy – Edgcumbes is a mecca for everyone who loves to enjoy freshly roasted coffee and loose-leaf tea.

A family business with many foodie facets, Edgcumbes Coffee Roasters & Tea Blenders has been going for mor than 35 years, with a simple love of coffee and tea at its heart. It was founded in 1981 by Frank Edgcumbe-Rendle, who, on returning from India where he had worked as a tea trader, was frustrated at the lack of good quality loose-leaf tea in the UK.

Today the business is headed up by his daughter-in-law Alice, with the help of her husband Christopher and, when they are passing through, their four sons. In 2015, the roastery moved to a converted Dutch barn, acquired a beautiful Dutch coffee roaster – and named her Big Bertha!

Edgcumbes has expanded and evolved in its new home to become a real hub of the community. They opened an on-site café and shop two years ago to showcase their products. From its peaceful location near the Sussex coast, the café has become a haven for tea and coffee enthusiasts.

From walkers and cyclists to 'in-the-know' locals who love to watch the coffee being roasted, Alice describes the café as being for absolutely everyone and anyone. Using one word to describe what makes their coffee special, Alice would say, "fresh". No coffee in the shop or café is over 1 week old; a world away from the coffee you buy in supermarkets.

At the end of 2017 the café moves into new larger premises, and the team begin serving savoury dishes alongside their popular sweet menu. Everything will still be homemade, whether on the premises or from a local producer. Once customers have enjoyed their drink in the café, they can pop through to the shop to buy some coffee or loose-leaf tea to take home, as well as the essential brewing equipment.

As part of their commitment to sustainability, the shop offers an innovative scheme where people can bring their own tin to fill up with coffee or tea. This not only saves on packaging, but allows Edgcumbes to keep producing premium quality at really fair prices.

Alice and the team love sharing their enthusiasm for, and knowledge of, coffee and tea with their guests, which leads us on to the final facet of Edgcumbes – the inspiring food and craft academy. Here people can enjoy courses on coffee, baking, chocolate-making and even crafting cards from coffee sacks, in a specially designed space converted from a former cattle stable.

You can visit Edgcumbes any day of the week and you can also buy online at www.edgcumbes.co.uk.

BURUNDI
GIHERE

EDGE
by Edgcumbes

Caffeine Addicts

ROASTED Coffee

SPECIALITY BLENDS

SUSSEX BARN
RIVERSIDE ESPRESSO
DARK SIDE OF THE EDGE

MICRO-LOTS

SINGLE ORIGIN
BRAZIL - RIO VERDE
COLOMBIA - LA PALELLA
ETHIOPA - YIRGACHEFFE
ETHIOPA - SIDAMO
KENYA - KISII PB
GUATEMALA

SWISS WATER DECAF
Bright Acidity, Fine

Lemon & Ginger
Ceylon
£5·30 100g

English
Breakfast
Orthodox
£3·70 100g

Keenum China
Black
£4·95 100g

Edgcumbes

Edgcumbes

Coffee
& Tea
Takeaway

Roastery
Shop

OPEN
Monday - Friday
7am to 5pm

Saturday - Sunday
9:30am to 4pm

Edgcumbes
MOCHA STOUT CAKE

A sublime marriage of freshly brewed coffee, hand-crafted beer and chocolate – this is a knockout in our Edge Café! You can adapt the topping as you wish. Cream cheese, frosted icing or buttercream icing are just as delicious!

Prep time: 20 minutes | Cook time: 1 hour | Makes: 12 squares

Ingredients

For the cake:

150ml Edgcumbes cold brew coffee (we used our award-winning Sussex Barn Coffee Beans)

100ml stout (we used Arundel Brewery Sussex Dark Stout)

250g unsalted butter

75g unsweetened cocoa powder

400g caster sugar

140ml soured cream or buttermilk

2 large free-range eggs

1 tbsp vanilla extract

275g plain flour

2½ tsp bicarbonate of soda

For the topping:

550g icing sugar

300g unsalted butter, cut into cubes

Freshly roasted coffee beans, to decorate

Method

For the cake

Preheat the oven to fan 160°c. Butter and fully line a 23cm/9 inch loose-based square tin or a 23cm/9 inch spring-form round tin.

Pour the cold brew and stout into a large saucepan and add the butter. Heat through until all the butter is melted. Whisk in the cocoa and sugar. Beat the soured cream (or buttermilk) and eggs together with the vanilla extract. Then add the egg mixture to the pan of coffee and stout, and finally whisk in the flour and bicarbonate of soda, either by hand or with an electric whisk.

Pour the mixture (which should resemble a loose batter) into the greased and lined tin and bake for 45 minutes to 1 hour, depending on your oven. If looking 'not yet cooked', but getting crispy on top, wet a sheet of baking parchment and place over the top of the tin in the oven, which will protect the top and sides of the cake.

When cooked, leave the cake to cool in the tin on a cooling rack. Once cool, lift out and allow to cool completely.

For the topping

Now make the icing. Put the icing sugar in a food processor and blitz, as this will remove any lumps without the need to sieve.

Add the butter, cut into cubes, and blitz again until it is a spreadable consistency. Spread on to the top of the cake to form a nice thick topping resembling a latte or cappuccino. Decorate sparingly with freshly roasted coffee beans!

Best of the BRUNCH

Friendly neighbourhood café Egg & Spoon has become a favourite amongst Kemptown locals thanks to its hearty food and warm welcome.

Set at the heart of the residential neighbourhood of Kemptown village, Egg & Spoon is a relaxed café serving up breakfast, brunch and lunch to its hordes of loyal customers seven days a week. It was set up by husband and wife team Fran and Ben, who met while working at Mildred's in Soho. Before opening their café, they spent years on the road catering on music tours – feeding the likes of Coldplay, Foo Fighters, Joan Baez, Willie Nelson, Norah Jones, Justin Timberlake, Muse and Gorillaz.

They established their catering business, Egg & Spoon, in 2006. After nine successful years and hundreds of private dinner parties, festivals, corporate weekenders, weddings and pop-ups, they decided it was time to create their own base in their beloved Brighton, and opened their café in 2015.

Everything is made from scratch in the café – they salt their own beef, make their own baked beans and their own granola, for example. What they don't make on-site, they buy from as near as possible. The bread comes from Real Patisserie and the sausages travel just a few doors down the street from their butchers, Bramptons.

As well as the plentiful breakfast and brunch options (including mouth-watering vegan and vegetarian dishes), they are known for their hot sandwich specials at lunchtime. They have four or five regulars, plus the occasional special, for example the beloved Texican (recipe overleaf) or the Cuban (made with delicious pulled pork).

Everything is cooked to order, and this commitment to quality saw them win Best Café at the Brighton Food and Drink awards in 2016, just a year after opening. With around 90% of their customers being regulars, Fran and Ben are now dedicated to maintaining this award-winning food and service. It has built a reputation for its warm welcome – children are always welcome in the café, as are four-legged friends.

Despite the success of the café, Fran and Ben haven't quite left the catering arm of Egg & Spoon behind just yet. They regularly host pop-ups in the café, as well as hiring it out for events. They can also be found catering for private parties, events and, occasionally, weddings. They especially love catering dinner parties in people's own homes – the perfect way to enjoy the relaxed environment of your own home, without the washing up!

Egg & Spoon
TEXICAN

The salt beef quantities will make too much for this recipe, but it's worth making it in a larger quantity and freezing the rest.

Preparation time: 1 hour, plus 10 days brining | Cooking time: 6 hours | Serves 4

Ingredients

For the salt beef:

1kg beef brisket

4 litres water

500g salt

250g light brown sugar

5 bay leaves

1 star anise

1 tbsp coriander seeds

½ tbsp each of cumin seeds, chilli flakes, juniper berries and black peppercorns

½ bulb garlic, skin and all, broken up

For the pickled red onion:

1 medium red onion

2 tsp salt

1 lemon, juiced

For the chipotle sauce:

2 tomatoes

2 red peppers

20g coriander

20g flat leaf parsley

50g tomato purée

1 clove garlic

½ tin chipotle chillies

1 lemon, zested and juiced

Salt and pepper

For the garlic mayo:

½ bulb garlic

50g parsley, chopped

100g good-quality mayonnaise

To assemble:

4 brioche buns, toasted

Sliced jalapeño peppers

40g rocket

Method

For the salt beef

Cut the brisket into four or five pieces and place in a deep plastic container with a fitted lid (approx. 6 litre capacity). Place all the remaining ingredients for the salt beef in a large pan to make the brine. Bring to the boil, stir to check the sugar and salt have dissolved, and then leave to cool completely. Once cooled, cover the brisket with the brine. You may need to weigh the brisket down to keep it covered – we use filled teacups or water bottles. Refrigerate for at least 10 days.

Remove the brisket from the brine, rinse and place into a large pan. Cover with water and simmer on a low heat for 5 hours. Leave to cool for an hour or so in the pan, remove the brisket and shred the meat using a couple of forks.

For the pickled red onion

Slice the onion as finely as you can. Place in a small bowl, sprinkle the onion with salt and mix in the lemon juice. Refrigerate for a couple of hours, then squeeze the onions and discard the juice.

For the chipotle sauce

Preheat the oven to 220°c. Roast the tomatoes and peppers together in the oven until soft, leave to cool then remove the skins. Blend with all the other ingredients in a mixer until they form a thick paste.

For the garlic mayo

Preheat the oven to 160°c. Wrap the garlic in foil, drizzled with olive oil & sprinkled with salt. Roast for an hour or so until soft. When cooled, squeeze the garlic from the skins, add to the parsley and mayonnaise and blitz in a mixer until blended.

To assemble

Reheat 400g of the salt beef in a frying pan on a low/medium heat until hot. Slice the brioche buns in half and toast the insides lightly under the grill. Spread a generous spoonful of chipotle sauce on the bottom halves and top with the salt beef. Pile a good forkful of pickled red onions and two or three slices of jalapeño on top of the salt beef and return under the grill briefly. Spread a good dollop of garlic mayo on the top halves of the buns, add a handful of rocket and place on the bottoms. Serve.

Culinary CREATIVITY

The first restaurant from MasterChef: The Professionals winner Steven Edwards, etch. is a celebration of locality, seasonality and creativity.

Chef Steven Edwards rose to culinary fame when he was crowned one of the youngest ever winners of MasterChef: The Professionals in 2013. A talented chef, he had long dreamed of owning his own restaurant. With the coveted win behind him and praise from the likes of Michel Roux Jr., Steven saw the opportunity to make his dream a reality.

He stayed at five-star country house hotel South Lodge, where he had been part of the team since 2008, for a further year following his MasterChef appearance, before embarking on his own culinary journey. He began with a series of pop-ups, where he aimed to find his style and decide where he could see himself basing his own eatery.

He chose Church Road in Hove thanks to the inspiring foodie culture of the city. Although there are many great places to eat in Brighton and Hove, there was a bit of a gap in the market for high-end restaurants. With his restaurant, etch., Steven intended to provide the fine dining experience, but to strip it right back to reflect his age and create an unpretentious experience.

The restaurant itself is a reflection of this aim, with its exposed features and slightly industrial, distressed feel. The open kitchen and bar provide unrestricted views of the food being cooked and the cocktails being made.

The menu itself reads as a list of almost cryptic clues. Steven describes each dish in a couple of words so customers are not baffled with long descriptions. Luckily the knowledgeable front of house staff taste the menu each week and can explain the menu to diners in their own words. They can tell you everything from how it is cooked to where the ingredients were sourced.

Steven works closely with bar manager Sam to develop the menus alongside the weekly changing wine list. Matching wine flights are available for each tasting menu to complement the food. With the help of restaurant manager Sophia, the whole experience – food, drinks, service and atmosphere – come together to create a unique dining experience focusing on the bounty of the surrounding county… this is Sussex on a plate.

etch
SEA TROUT WITH CUCUMBER SORBET

A stunning recipe by MasterChef: The Professionals 2013 winner,
Steven Edwards, from his restaurant etch. You will need an ice cream machine,
a blowtorch and a vacpac machine to create all the components
of this beautiful dish.

Preparation time: 1 hour, plus freezing, compressing and curing time| Cooking time: 15 minutes | Serves 10

Ingredients

For the trout:
1 side of sea trout (600g)

100g caster sugar

100g table salt

Oil, for coating

For the tartare:
25g capers

1g parsley, chopped

2g chives, chopped

¼ banana shallot, diced

30g ketchup

5g Worcestershire sauce

30g mayo

15 wholegrain mustard

For the sorbet:
190ml cucumber juice, from 1 whole cucumber

15g caster sugar

10g ProSorbet

For the compressed and torched cucumber:
1 cucumber

Salt

For the cucumber ketchup:
1 cucumber, chopped

½ onion, chopped

½ green pepper, deseeded and chopped

100g water

80g white wine vinegar

2g agar

3g salt

40g caster sugar

Method

For the cured and flamed trout

Scale and pin-bone the sea trout (you can get the fishmonger to do this for you). Use half of the trout to cut 10 rectangles, 30g each. Set aside the remaining half for the tartare. Mix together the sugar and salt. Roll the trout portions in the mixture to coat. Place on a tray and refrigerate for 45 minutes, then rinse gently under cold water. Lay on a clean J-cloth to dry. Rub with oil, place on an oven tray and blowtorch the skin until dark and crispy.

For the trout tartare

Finely dice the reserved trout. Mix together the capers, parsley, chives, shallot, ketchup, Worcestershire sauce, mayo and mustard. Just before serving, mix the sea trout into the tartare sauce.

For the sorbet

Juice the whole cucumber using a juicing machine. You will get approximately 200ml of juice from it; you will need 190ml of juice for the recipe. Heat 100ml of the cucumber juice with the caster sugar and stir to dissolve. Once dissolved, add the remaining 90ml of juice and the ProSorbet, a stabiliser available online, and whisk to combine. Add the mixture to an ice cream machine to churn and freeze. Use the sorbet within 2 hours of freezing. It can be used after this time, but it may need defrosting and re-churning to make soft.

For the compressed and torched cucumber

Peel the cucumber, vacuum pack and place in the fridge for 12 hours. Quarter lengthways, remove the seeds and portion into squares (for the compressed) and rectangles (for the torched). Oil the rectangles and season with sea salt. Blowtorch and set aside for plating.

For the cucumber ketchup

Combine the cucumber, onion, pepper and water in a pan. Cook until tender and all the water has evaporated. Blitz until smooth, then add the vinegar, salt and sugar and boil again. Add the agar and boil again. Remove from the heat and leave to cool in the fridge until set. Blitz again until smooth, then store in a piping bag ready to plate.

Passion for PROVENANCE

From a small herd of pedigree pigs to a thriving independent business featuring a butcher's shop, butchery courses and event catering, Wild Garlic Farm is passionate about conservation, farming and preserving our native breeds.

Garlic Wood Farm began life when Paul Martin took his passion for conservation farming and decided to turn it into his day job. He left his advertising career in London behind in 2010 and began a family business with a small herd of Gloucester Old Spot pigs. It all started through the simple passion for preserving native and rare breeds and for farming in a truly sustainable way.

The young business was named Garlic Wood Farm after the woodland on the farmland, which is carpeted in fragrant wild garlic. The pigs were soon joined by Southdown sheep, as well as Highland cattle, which grazed on a National Trust nature reserve.

From its beginnings, selling at local farmers' markets, Garlic Wood Farm was soon so successful they were able to open their own high street shop in Steyning. Since the business has grown, their own farming enterprise has returned to being the small-scale hobby it started out as. They now work with other farmers who share their approach to conserving traditional breeds to bring a variety of native, slow-matured, naturally fed livestock to the shop. This allows them to widen their range of produce and to ensure consistency of supply. In the traditional butcher's shop, they butcher the whole carcass on-site and dry-age the beef on the bone for at least 28 days.

They share this passion for field-to-fork quality in their butchery courses, which are run from their cutting room. "Lots of our customers are really interested in where their food comes from," explains Paul, "so our butchery courses teach them about the meat and what to do with it." Guests will certainly get hands-on during the course – from cutting and boning meat to rolling and tying joints for cooking.

Catering and events manager Toby heads up the catering side of Garlic Wood Farm. From large weddings to special dinners for two, every event is catered with the same philosophy in mind – great catering starts with great ingredients. Working with their artisan producers, Toby creates a bespoke menu for each event, featuring native breeds of pork, lamb, beef, game or poultry. Whether it's a hog roast, barbecue or elegant sharing table, the renowned Garlic Wood quality and taste is guaranteed.

Minted
Lamb
£2 each

Garlic Wood Farm

Garlic Wood Farm Butchery
PORCHETTA WITH SALSA VERDE

This is our take on the classic Italian street food dish. It's a simple meal packed with all the flavour of herb-stuffed free-range pork, fennel, garlic and just a hint of chilli. It was inspired by Toby's time living in Italy and now forms the centrepiece of our 'sharing plate' wedding celebration menu, as well as being a firm street food favourite at festivals and fairs.

Preparation time: 30 minutes | Cooking time: 2½ hours | Serves 4-6

Ingredients

For the porchetta:

2.5kg boneless loin and belly of free-range pork, well scored (ask your butcher to remove the skin where the belly and loin will overlap so that when it's rolled, the skin won't be inside the joint)

100g sea salt

30g cracked black pepper

30g ground fennel seeds

20g dried rosemary

15g dried chilli flakes

1 large bunch of parsley

1 bunch of fresh rosemary

fresh fennel tops

1 lemon, zested

3–4 cloves garlic, crushed

For the salsa verde:

2 large bunches of parsley

5 cloves garlic, crushed

½ tsp ground coriander

½ tsp ground fennel seeds

1 lemon, zested and juiced

Dried chilli flakes, or freshly chopped chilli to taste

Olive oil, as needed

Method

For the porchetta

Preheat the oven to 240°c/475°f/gas mark 9. Open out the pork loin, butterflying the eye of the loin in order to create a pocket for the stuffing.

Combine the salt, pepper, fennel seeds, dried rosemary and chilli flakes to make a dry rub mixture. Set aside. Roughly chop and mix the parsley, rosemary, fennel tops, lemon zest and crushed garlic to create the herb stuffing.

Sprinkle some of the dry rub mix on the surface of the meat. Add the herb stuffing mix evenly to the inside of the joint and then roll tightly and tie with butcher's string to create a joint.

Rub a generous amount of the dry rub onto the skin of the joint, ensuring it gets into every score mark. Place in a roasting tray and cook in the preheated oven for 25 minutes to set the crackling.

Turn the oven down to 180°c/350°f/gas mark 4 and continue to cook for 25 minutes per 1lb (50 minutes per kg), until the pork is cooked through and any juices run clear, (use a meat thermometer to check for an internal temperature of 75°c.)

For the salsa verde

Very finely chop the parsley and add to a small bowl with the crushed garlic, coriander, fennel, lemon juice and zest. Add enough olive oil to make a rough-textured salsa, and add the chilli to taste.

To serve

When the meat is cooked, remove it from the oven and leave to rest for 15-20 minutes before slicing the porchetta and serving with perfect crispy crackling and a helping of the salsa verde.

Artisans CHEESES

Best of BRITISH

A treasure trove of artisan cheeses, charcuterie and wine from across the country, The Great British Charcuterie Co. showcases the very best of British produce.

Situated at Brighton Marina, The Great British Charcuterie Company was opened in 2016 by father and son team Phil and Simon Bartley. A chef of 15 years, Phil was passionate about the plethora of incredible produce available locally and wanted to help to raise awareness of the talented artisan makers who create such amazing things on our doorstep.

British cheese had long been famed worldwide, but it was the emerging area of British charcuterie and English wine that inspired Phil and Simon to champion the unique range of products being made within the UK. Just a year after opening, they now boast the largest range of British cheeses, charcuterie and wines in the country.

Animal welfare is central to the ethos of the business. They passionately believe that happy animals make a superior product, and this view is shared by all of their suppliers. For this reason, they are able to bring together a collection of some of the tastiest British cheeses, charcuterie and wine – which can certainly rival Europe's famous offerings.

The friendly shop has built up a reputation for its helpful and informative approach. Manager Jack is usually on hand to advise customers on the products and offer them tastings to make sure they pick something they will love.

Their famous Charcoal Cheddar (the country's first and only black cheese, made in Yorkshire) has acquired a loyal following thanks to its jet-black colour and beautifully soft texture. "It is our best-selling product by a country mile," says Jack, "and it makes a great talking point on a cheeseboard."

When it comes to the charcuterie, it is hard to beat the award-winning air-dried Mangalitza Ham, which comes from Beal's Farm in Sussex. Customers also rave about the Beer Sticks (which are made from Sussex pork at Moons Green, and are perfect with an English beer), the Cornish Chorizo and the incredible Highland Wagyu.

Alongside regular tasting evenings, customers can now take a seat in the shop and try a charcuterie or cheese plate along with a glass of English wine; the perfect setting to enjoy the relaxed atmosphere of the shop alongside a taste of some of the country's finest produce.

The Great British Charcuterie Co.

AIR DRIED HAM
MONMOUTHSHIRE
TREALY FARM WALES
100g £6.00

SMOKED AIR DRIED
HAM
SUSSEX

AIR DRIED BEEF
MONMOUTHSHIRE
TREALY FARM
100g £6.00

WALNUT
RYE
£2.35

RUSTIC
LOAF
£1.60

WHITE
SOURDOUGH
£1.65

Great British Charcuterie Co.
THE PERFECT SUSSEX DELI BOARD

Whether for a light lunch or a dinner party, it is hard to beat a delicious selection of farmhouse cheeses and cured meats. We are incredibly lucky here to have some of the country's best cheese and charcuterie producers right on our doorstep. With so many to choose from, this is designed to be a guide to help you create the perfect selection.

Preparation time: 15 minutes | Cooking time: 40 minutes | Serves 4

Ingredients

For the cheeses:

Aim for 60g per person for each cheese, and remove from the fridge 1 hour before serving to reach room temperature

Mayfield Swiss

Brighton Blue

Sussex Brie

Golden Cross

For the charcuterie:

Aim for 30g per person, thinly sliced

Air-dried Manglaitza Ham

South Downs Chorizo

Smoked Sussex Air-dried Ham

South Downs Fennel Salami

For the accompaniments:

Good-quality bread, such as sourdough

A selection of artisan biscuits

Piccalilli

Peach chutney

Pickled onions

Salted butter

Gherkins

Method

Choosing your cheeses

When selecting cheese for your board, a general rule is to include a hard cheese, a blue cheese, a soft cheese, and a goat's, ewe's milk or washed-rind cheese. For the hard cheese, we have selected Mayfield Swiss, a wonderfully nutty cheese with a creamy texture from Sussex cheese makers Alsop & Walker. For the blue cheese, we have gone with the fantastic Brighton Blue, a mild-tasting blue with piquant blue veins. For the soft cheese, we've chosen another fantastic cheese from Alsop & Walker, their mushroomy-tasting Sussex Brie. For the goat's cheese, we couldn't think of a better cheese than Golden Cross, a soft, full-flavoured goat's cheese that is rolled in ash to help mature the cheese. If you wanted to go for ewe's milk cheese, Golden Cross make the fantastic Flower Marie, or for a washed-rind cheese try Burwash Rose from the Traditional Cheese Dairy. A pungent cheese with a mild, fruity flavour, this cheese is washed daily in rose water during production.

Choosing your charcuterie

There are no real rules here, however we suggest aiming for a variety of salamis and whole muscles, such as hams or bresaolas, to showcase the fantastic range of cured meats available in Sussex. Starting with our salamis, we went with two outstanding ones from Calcot farm: their Fennel Salami, made with free-range Sussex pork and just the right amount of fennel so the flavour isn't too overpowering and the stunning South Downs Chorizo. A great take on the Spanish favourite full of smoked paprika. This provides the softer textures for the board. To add a different texture, we have gone with Smoked Sussex Air-dried Ham, a great ham that is first air-dried then expertly smoked. To finish, we couldn't leave out the superb Mangalitza Ham from Beal's farm in Chailey, made from the leg of their own rare-breed Mangalitza pork, famed for its rich flavour and marbled fat.

Choosing your accompaniments

Choosing the right accompaniments can lift your deli board and make it one to remember. It's always worth going for the best you can find; your delicious cheeses and charcuterie deserve no less. When it comes to the perfect accompaniments for cheese, you can't go far wrong with a good helping of chutney. We suggest two chutneys to pair with your cheeses. We've chosen the ever-versatile piccalilli, great with hard cheeses, and the slightly more unusual peach chutney, which works wonders with blue and creamier cheeses. Pickled fruits and veg make a great addition, too, as the acidity helps cleanse the palate after the richness of the cheese. For your charcuterie, less is more. Strong chutneys or pickles can overpower the delicate flavours of the meats, so keep it simple – cornichons are a great choice. Last but not least, breads, crackers and biscuits add texture and give you something to put it all on. A good quality sourdough or farmhouse bread from one of Sussex's many fantastic artisan bakeries is a must, and always go for a selection of crackers, from the plain natural crackers to the crowd-pleasing buttermilk toasts for cheese.

Supermarket REVOLUTION

hiSbe is a supermarket breaking the mould – a social enterprise business that puts people and communities first.

When sisters Amy and Ruth Anslow wanted to challenge the way the food system worked, it all came down to one phrase… "how it should be", which gave the name hiSbe to their exciting new idea. hiSbe is a supermarket that follows a social enterprise model, which means they pay producers and charge customers what is fair, not what maximises profit.

The idea that people should be able to buy great quality food at more affordable prices has driven hiSbe from the start. This concept goes hand in hand with providing honest information about the products, especially where they have come from and how they were sourced. There is an equal commitment to fair pricing and fair trading, as well as paying all staff above the Living Wage Foundation's living wage.

Whether it's fresh fruit and veg, dairy products, meat, fish, bread or store cupboard essentials, hiSbe prioritises small, local producers and brands that trade responsibly. They avoid excess food packaging by using dispensers for a variety of dry foods, and by selling most fruit and veg loose by weight. This means customers can buy as much or as little as they like, avoid food waste, reduce packaging waste and reuse containers.

Amy and Ruth describe the hiSbe way: "At hiSbe we think that putting happiness first is a route to a more fair, responsible and sustainable food industry. So, we consider the happiness of people, animals and the planet in our sourcing, decision making and the way we do business." For every pound spent at hiSbe around 50p stays in the local economy (compared to just 5p of a pound spent in a national supermarket). An average of 68p of every pound spent at hiSbe is paid to suppliers and producers (at the big supermarkets this is more like an estimated 7-10p).

The success of the shop on York Place has been nothing short of incredible since it opened in 2013. Open until 8pm, it offers a unique shopping experience that is also convenient for customers who work during the day. Amy and Ruth have been hatching plans to open more stores locally following the success of its first site. You can follow hiSbe on Facebook, Twitter and Instagram for updates on their progress.

hiSbe - Silo
CAULIFLOWER STEAK WITH MUSHROOM RISOTTO

This recipe has been provided by Silo. A zero-waste restaurant that serves pure foods born from clean farming. All the ingredients are available from hiSbe. This is a vegan game changer. Its robust meaty quality will convert the most resilient of carnivores. The beauty of the cauliflower 'tree of life' presentation makes it the ultimate dinner party showstopper.

Preparation time: 10 minutes | Cooking time: 1 hour | Serves 4-6

Ingredients

For the mushroom risotto:

600g button mushrooms

2 litres water

Soy sauce (optional)

300g short-grain brown rice

50g brown rice miso paste

Rapeseed oil, for cooking

For the cauliflower steak:

3 medium-large cauliflowers

To garnish:

100g lemon thyme, leaves picked

Method

For the mushroom risotto

The stock should be your first job as it takes about an hour. Roughly slice the mushrooms and sweat in rapeseed oil over a high heat in a heavy-based pan. Cook until golden brown. Add the water, bring to a simmer and leave for 40-50 minutes until it tastes very mushroomy. If you have the stalks from the lemon thyme, you can add these too. Strain off the mushroom slices to use in another dish. (The mushroom stock leaches all the flavour from the mushrooms. The mushrooms can now be used to thicken a soup or go into a curry for nice chunky texture. Zero waste.)

Reduce the mushroom liquid until it tastes quite intense. Season with soy sauce to make it even more intense, if you like. It needs to be strong, as the rice and cauliflower are quite neutral flavours.

Meanwhile boil the rice for about 20 minutes until it starts to break down and is very tender. Strain and reserve.

For the cauliflower steaks

Take all the outer leaves off the cauliflower and reserve for another use. Turn the head of cauliflower upside down and cut through the centre of the root directly down. Then cut the steak 2.5cm from the centre, parallel with your first cut. This will reveal a beautiful 'tree of life' steak. You will get two big steaks from one cauliflower. There will be a lot of cauliflower trim. The trimmings are ideal for a salad, soup or a vegan cauliflower curry.

Bring a suitably sized pan of water to a simmer. Season the water, it should taste slightly salty. To be really precise, the salt should be 5% of the weight of the water. Poach the steaks until tender. This can be done ahead of time.

To serve

Heat the plates up. Ideally your serving plate will be slightly concave so that the stock/sauce doesn't run across the plate. Put the rice in a heavy-based pot with half of the mushroom liquid and season with the brown rice miso paste. Gently warm, but don't boil. The more you beat this mixture the more glutinous the risotto will become.

To warm the steaks up, deep fry them for 90 seconds at 180°c. Alternatively, place in a steamer or neatly lay them into a pan with a lid on and a small amount of water, until they are hot.

Spoon 3 large tablespoons of risotto into the base of each warmed plate. Sprinkle the lemon thyme leaves around the edges of the risotto. Place the steaks neatly on the centre of the risotto. Finish by neatly drizzling the remains of the mushroom stock/sauce around the edge of the risotto. Voila!

Innovative FINE DINING

From a two-day-a-week pop-up to a nationally acclaimed fine-dining experience, Isaac At is breaking down traditional barriers between chefs and diners one step at a time.

Isaac At was started by chef Isaac Bartlett-Copeland in the spring of 2015. The restaurant began life as an original pop-up in an old office space, which Isaac had converted to accommodate his vision. The 32-cover pop-up was an intimate dining experience that aimed to push the boundaries of fine dining to give diners something a little different, while being the first to focus on a Sussex-inspired menu across both food and drink.

A warm interior welcomed the guests to the converted dining room. Being tucked away in a low-footfall area, but in the heart of the North-Laine, Isaac put an emphasis on pre-booking, which allowed him to create a relaxed dining experience for everyone.

The ever-changing menu is inspired by the bounty of the county, from the farmland to the Sussex coastline, so that a visit to Isaac At is to experience a true taste of the south coast. The menu changes according to the season and depends entirely on availability of ingredients, which are sourced daily. The team work collaboratively to push the boundaries of every dish they create, using new cooking techniques to create bold flavours.

This commitment to local sourcing doesn't stop when it comes to the drinks list either. In an unusual achievement, Isaac At is the only restaurant in Brighton to have crafted a drinks list that is exclusively English, with a fantastic array of wines, beers and spirits from Sussex itself.

Isaac At relaunched as a permanent restaurant in the summer of 2016, opening as a five-day-a-week 20-cover dining experience, following a renovation. As the team has expanded and the restaurant has evolved, it has gone on to win awards across the city, as well as being named in the Good Food Guide.

Despite the culinary accolades and national recognition, for Isaac, there is no such thing as arriving at a culinary destination. For Isaac and his team, Isaac At will always be an ever-evolving work in progress, as they continue to learn, explore and experiment in the kitchen, and be inspired by the landscape around them.

Isaac At

PORK NECK WITH SMOKED CELERIAC PURÉE, PICKLED APPLE AND NASTURTIUM LEAVES

Creamy and smoky celeriac purée, flavoursome pickled apple and melt-in-the-mouth pork neck. It takes over 36 hours to prepare the pork neck and 10 hours to make the sauce, so this dish needs to be started in advance.

Preparation time: 12 hours | Cooking time: 24 hours, plus 3 hours cooling and setting | Serves 4

Ingredients

For the pork neck:

1 litre water

120g salt

10 black peppercorns

10 cloves

½ pork neck

500g pork skin

Butter, for frying

For the sauce:

1kg pork bones

2 litres water

For the celeriac purée:

Small bunch of hay

50ml cream

1 celeriac

Salt and pepper

For the pickled apple:

50ml white wine vinegar

50ml granulated sugar

1 Granny Smith apple

To serve:

6 nasturtium leaves, foraged or grown in the garden

Method

For the pork neck

Heat the water, then add the salt, peppercorns and cloves to make a brine, and leave to cool before adding the pork neck to prevent cooking the meat. Leave to soak for 12 hours.

Take out of the brine and lightly rinse the neck under fresh water. Roll the neck meat in pork skin (the collagen in the skin keeps the pork moist) and wrap in cling film to keep the round shape. Vacuum pack the pork neck and place in a water bath at 65°c for 24 hours.

To cool the neck, take it out of the bath and rest for 30 minutes. Run the sealed bag under cold water for 30 minutes, then transfer to ice water for another 30 minutes. Move to the fridge to let it set for 2 hours.

Remove from the fridge and peel off the skin. Carve into 150g disks. When ready to serve, fry them in a hot pan with a knob of butter.

For the sauce

Preheat the oven to 150°c. Roast the bones and any pork trim in the oven for 4 hours until all the meat has no moisture and is heavily caramelised (not burnt). Put the bones and trim in a pan with the water, bring to just under simmering and cook for 10 hours. Strain the stock then reduce until you have a light glaze.

For the celeriac purée

Get a large pan with a lid and place the hay around the outside. Put the cream in a cup and place in the middle. Light the hay. Cover with the pan lid and let the hay burn out (we recommend you do this outside or away from a fire alarm).

Peel, roughly dice and slice down the celeriac. Add to the pan of boiling water and cook for 5 minutes. Drain and blend. Pass the purée through a sieve and combine with the smoked cream. Season to taste.

For the pickled apple

Heat the vinegar and sugar together, then leave to cool. Dice half the apple and juice the other half, and add both to the gastrique (the vinegar and sugar mixture.) Vacuum pack and leave until needed.

To serve

Fry off the pork neck and serve with the celeriac purée, pickled apple and sauce. Garnish with nasturtium leaves.

Introducing
MARWOOD

Thanks to the struggle to find a decent coffee with a bit of banter, Marwood Bar & Coffee House was opened in a perfect storm of a recession and some blind faith.

After many years of travel and adventure, founder Rich Grills returned to England in June 2006 ready for a new challenge. 'The budget for Marwood was the smell of an oily rag.' So, no budget. And no idea. They borrowed a van, skip-dipped, cleared the folks' loft out of old toys, begged and bartered. The name took a while to be decided. After dismissing a series of bad grinding puns, they had a few beers and watched Withnail and I for the thousandth time. Marwood is "I" from the film, so it doesn't mean anything to most people.

Eight years down the line and Marwood guests can hire the space exclusively, the venue hosts huge parties and a variety of events year round, including fundraisers and quirky community based offerings. You can also enjoy the same lovingly made coffee, a cold craft beer or an Aperol Spritz in the cocktail bar. There's delicious food available and after winning Most Brighton Venue in the 2017 Bravo awards, you wouldn't want to miss a chance to visit this hidden gem.

Something a little
DIFFERENT

A second venture from the owners of Marwood, Presuming Ed Coffee House shares much in common with its sister venue, but also has a unique identity of its own.

Situated in an old bank, in October of 2014, the team once again began skip-raiding and building the café from scratch. The London Road location remains a beacon of home-grown, un-gentrified community, probably the last in Brighton.

With a lot of help from the council, the beautiful old building was transformed into a craft coffee house, to include a 12-seater micro cinema, laptop workstations and a gorgeous beer garden. Although also named after a character in Withnail and I, it's a different creature to Marwood; grittier, edgier, more home-grown. Like a bolshie younger sister who's trying to be a grown-up but hasn't quite got the hang of it yet.

If you like Marwood, you'll love Presuming Ed Coffee House. Stop by for a beer sometime and check out a film in the cinema.

Marwood Bar & Coffeehouse
THE LEMON BONBON

Invented by the Dragon, a man whose bartending prowess is so legendary it's rumoured he is the love child of King Arthur and Lady Godiva … and Merlin is his Godfather. He is a man of infinite knowledge and even more hats. He has a penchant for baking aprons and can often be found behind the counter at Marwood yelling at customers with a megaphone. You don't meet The Dragon … The Dragon meets you.

The neo-retro classic cocktail is so simple that it's impossible to get wrong, and if you do, then hang your head in shame and retire from mixing drinks forever. This drink is not something that you can rush and needs at least six days of advanced preparation, so bear in mind this isn't something you can bash out 30 minutes before a dinner party.

Preparation time: 6 days | Serves 6

Ingredients

For the Werther's vodka (makes 16-18 drinks):

Approximately 250g of Werther's Original butter sweets (do not get the ones that are filled; you want the original hard ones that chip teeth)

1 bottle of vodka (we use No 9 Small Batch Vodka)

For the sugar syrup:

1 cup (approx. 200g) golden caster sugar

For the cocktail:

300ml Werther's vodka

150ml fresh lemon juice

75ml sugar syrup

Ice

Method

Day 1

Fill an air-tight 1 litre glass jar with the sweets. It works best if you unwrap each sweet.

Pour the vodka into the jar (keep the empty bottle), seal the jar and store in a cupboard.

Day 2

Shake the jar and stir gently with a spoon. The sweets should be stuck together at the bottom. Don't worry too much about this. Seal the jar and store again.

Day 3, 4 and 5

Shake the jar, stir gently and seal again each day.

Day 6 – drinks day

You have your vodka! Pour it into a measuring jug. There might be some small sweets at bottom of jar left, again don't worry too much about this. Now slowly pour the vodka back into the empty bottle you kept. Your vodka will have increased approximately 10-15% in volume, so there should be some left in the measuring jug, which is great as now you can use this to make some drinks!

For the sugar syrup

Take the golden caster sugar and measure out a cup of sugar into a small pan, ideally something like a milk pan. Fill the same cup with water and add to pan. Put the pan on a low heat and stir occasionally, not allowing the mixture to boil, until you have a 1:1 sugar syrup (equal quantities of water to sugar).

For the cocktail

Get 6 rocks glasses ready, then measure the cocktail ingredients into a cocktail shaker. Seal the cocktail shaker and do your best Tom Cruise (if you don't get the reference, immediately purchase and watch the film Cocktail). Fill the rocks glasses with ice. Pour Lemon Bonbon equally between the glasses. Garnish with a thick slice of lemon, add optional cocktail umbrella, drink and enjoy!

Your Werther's vodka will keep for about three weeks in a cool cupboard and each batch should make you approximately 16-18 drinks.

Presuming Ed's Coffeehouse
GLUTEN-FREE PEACH BELLINI CAKE

This is one of our signature life-changing Bundt cakes. A light and moist gluten-free sponge with Champagne Chantilly cream and fresh and dehydrated fruits.
Our life-changing cakes are made by next level baker, Lois.
Her recipes are so good we don't let her out of the kitchen in case she gets injured or decides to go on holiday, or have any babies.

Preparation time: 30 minutes | Cooking time: 30 minutes | Makes 8" Bundt cake or 10" round cake

Ingredients

For the cake:

360g gluten-free multipurpose flour (we use Dove's Farm)

1½ tsp gluten-free baking powder (we use Dove's Farm)

1 tsp gluten-free bicarbonate of soda (we use Dove's Farm)

2½ tsp chia seeds

7 tsp boiling water

145g unsalted butter

360g caster sugar

2½ tsp pure vanilla extract

5 eggs

145g Greek yogurt

1 small tin of peaches in light syrup, syrup reserved

For the peach syrup:

Syrup reserved from tinned peaches

75ml peach schnapps

For the Chantilly cream:

200ml double cream

2 tbsp caster sugar

Champagne essence, if desired (we use Cupcake World)

For the decorations:

We use dehydrated dried fruits, hand-painted with edible food dyes, which can be made with a dehydrator or a domestic oven. Alternatively, you can use fresh fruits and berries to give your cake a pop of colour.

Method

For the cake

Preheat oven to 190°c with the rack in the middle. Line the bottom and sides of a 25cm/10-inch cake tin or grease and flour (we use gluten-free flour here too) an 20cm/8-inch Bundt tin.

Combine the flour, baking powder and bicarbonate of soda together in a medium bowl.

In a small bowl, combine the chia seeds and boiling water. Mix and let it sit for a couple of minutes until a slurry forms. In a separate bowl, beat the butter and sugar until light and fluffy. Add the vanilla and eggs, and continue beating until very creamy and light in color. Add the chia seed mixture and Greek yogurt, then beat to combine.

Fold in the dry mixture, then layer the peach slices evenly on top. Bake until the cake turns golden, and the tester comes out clean; about 20-35 minutes, depending on your oven. If it's not done, return to the oven for 10-20 minutes until golden brown, set and a skewer comes out clean.

Allow the cake to cool (still in the baking pan) on a wire rack for about 40 minutes, then release the cake from the pan. At this point, if the cake is cool enough, you can slide your hand under the cake, between the parchment paper and the bottom portion of the spring-form pan, and move the cake with the parchment paper attached to its bottom onto a cake plate easily. Or transfer the Bundt cake on to a wire rack and allow to cool completely.

For the peach syrup

Reduce the peach syrup left over from the tinned peaches to about half its original volume, then add peach schnapps. Brush over the cooled sponge cake with a pastry brush.

For the Chantilly cream

Beat the cream and sugar with an electric whisk or hand-held beater until firm peaks form. Be careful not to over whip! Add a few drops of Champagne essence, if desired.

To decorate

Decorate by piping Chantilly cream on the cake and adding fresh fruits and berries.

COFFEE

Espresso
Macchiato
Picolo
Americano
Long Black
Flat White
Cappuccino
Latte
Mocha
Hot Choc

Guest

Vintage CHARMS

Describing themselves as a storm in a vintage teacup, Metrodeco is a sumptuous medley of afternoon tea, unique tea cocktails and vintage charm.

Metrodeco is owned by Maggie Morgan and Helen Taggart. Situated just outside the hub of Brighton centre, in Kemptown, they have worked extremely hard to make their venue a destination place. By bringing together their love of antiques (Maggie) and tea (Helen), they achieved success in the creation of their quirky, friendly, vintage tea room.

The vintage theme was created by Maggie's eye for interesting but stylish pieces, while Helen's passion for tea drove the creation of the tea list. The list comprises quality blends to suit a range of tastes and moods, which she felt was missing from any other venue in the city. Their tea company, mdtea, now sells to many other places throughout Brighton and Sussex, as well as further afield.

Starting off slowly, and only selling tea and cakes in the first six months, the business has grown over the years and adapted smoothly to demand to serve lunches, afternoon tea and alcohol. Specialising in their own blends of tea, the natural progression was to create a range of alcoholic tea cocktails, and these have proved extremely popular – especially accompanying an afternoon tea, for which they are renowned not just throughout the city but nationwide. The recipe overleaf is the newest addition to their list and created by Andy their cocktail and bar manager.

In fact, their reputation is so great that Metrodeco were asked to give their expert advice on an episode of The Hotel Inspector, which featured a hotel that wanted to set up an afternoon tea service.

They champion local producers for their afternoon tea treats, although their scones, which have always been a cause for conversation, are baked in-house. Their sensational cakes seem to defy gravity and have customers returning for more. They are also known for their speciality gins – and their gin flights and gin tastings are not to be missed.

Customers range from regulars who pop in with their well-behaved dogs to couples celebrating anniversaries. And, of course, there are always many birthdays to be enjoyed, as well as discerning (as they like to call them) hen parties. Because of the vintage theme, parties often come in dressed exquisitely in the style of a bygone era. (This is optional and can just be admired).

The staff, however, do follow this theme – headscarves and braces are de rigueur for the vintage-styled servers who wish to give every customer a special experience.

Metrodeco
CHILLITO TEA COCKTAIL

A unique and delicious take on a mojito, this cocktail comprises homemade chilli and mint-infused rum, fresh mint, sugar syrup and lime. You need to make the infused rum 24 hours in advance.

Preparation time: 10 minutes, plus 24 hours infusing | Serves 1

Ingredients

For the infused rum:

50g Some Like It Hot tea (chilli and mint tea)

2 red chillies

700 ml white rum

For the cocktail:

50ml infused rum (see above)

25ml sugar syrup

A few mint leaves

2 pieces of fresh lime

Crushed ice

Soda water, to top up

To garnish:

Piece of dehydrated lime

Mint leaf

Dehydrated or fresh chilli

Method

For the infused rum

Mix the ingredients for the infused rum and leave to infuse for 24 hours. (If you can't get hold of the tea, fresh mint and 4 chillies can be substituted.)

For the cocktail

Place the infused rum, sugar syrup, mint and lime into a cocktail shaker. Muddle the lime and mint and shake well. Strain into a cocktail glass or glass teacup containing some crushed ice. Top up with a little soda water.

To garnish

Garnish with dehydrated lime, mint leaf and a chilli. Serve.

Culinary CUSTODIANS

Bread, cheese and wine – this is the 'holy trinity' at the heart of Pallant of Arundel, a historic grocery and delicatessen in the heart of Arundel

Pallant of Arundel has recently celebrated its tenth anniversary under the ownership of Mark Robinson and Jonathan Brantigan, but it has been serving the town of Arundel for hundreds of years before that…

"We see ourselves as custodians of the shop," says Mark. "We are lucky enough to run it during its present era, and one day we will hand it over to its next owners." It's clear from their philosophy that this is a very special place indeed.

From its origins as a grocery, Mark and Jonathan have developed the shop's offerings to include a wealth of produce. The focus is on things that are interesting, good-quality and that aren't otherwise available in the area. They describe the 'holy trinity' as being bread, cheese and wine – and they certainly offer an exceptional range of these products.

Having worked at a variety of prestigious retailers, from Selfridges and Fortnum & Mason to French cheese specialist La Fromagerie, they had the knowledge and experience to complement their passion for good food and wine. They champion small producers where possible, and stock a great selection of wines, cheeses, hams and groceries from the area.

They are known for their hand-carved ham on the bone, which has a Great Taste Award to its name. However, they also seek out the finest food from around the world – think Spanish pata negra, Italian salami and French charcuterie.

When it comes to local produce, the offerings reflect the season. For example, the juicy tomatoes come from a local nursery and can be enjoyed throughout their long season. However, during winter you won't find tomatoes at Pallant of Arundel, as they will be focusing on the fresh bounty of the current season.

Coffee to go, handmade sandwiches and salads are popular during the day, especially at the weekend when the bustling shop is packed with hungry visitors. People come from far and wide to get their hands on one of the coveted sausage rolls – many customers say they are the best they have ever tasted!

With artisan bread from local bakers, a mouth-watering cheese counter and all manner of store-cupboard ingredients, Pallant of Arundel continues to be one of Sussex's most beautiful and interesting shopping experiences – a food-lover's paradise and a treasure trove of fine produce.

Pallant of Arundel

COME INSIDE FOR ...
FARMHOUSE CHEESES
Artisan Breads
LOCAL Pies, Scotch Eggs, Salads
makes for
Perfect Picnics
with
SUSSEX BEERS AND WINES

Pallant of Arundel

BAKED GOLDEN CROSS GOAT'S CHEESE AND TOMATOES ON SOURDOUGH TOAST

Enjoy sweet caramelised shallot and tomato with creamy baked goat's cheese, and the crunch of sourdough bread for texture – a perfect lunchtime dish for spring or summer.

Prep time: 10 minutes | Cook time: 30 minutes | Serves 2

Ingredients

350g cherry tomatoes (red, orange and yellow will make a pretty plate)

4 medium shallots

4 thyme sprigs

2 rosemary stems

4-5 tbsp good quality olive oil

1 Golden Cross goat's cheese, thickly sliced

2 large but thin slices of sourdough bread

Basil leaves and extra rosemary, to garnish

Salt and black pepper

Method

Preheat the oven to 200°c/gas mark 6.

Cut the cherry tomatoes in half and place into a bowl. Peel the shallots, cut them in half lengthways, separate their layers and add to the tomatoes. Pull off the thyme and rosemary leaves, and add them to the bowl with a couple of generous glugs of good quality olive oil; perhaps 4-5 tablespoons. Season with salt and black pepper, and place in a roasting tray. Bake in the hot oven for 20 minutes.

Meanwhile on a piece of oiled foil, place thick slices of the Golden Cross (about 3-4 slices per person). Loosely pull the edges of the foil together to form a parcel, then scrunch the edges together to seal. After the tomatoes have been cooking for 20 minutes, add the foil parcel to the tomatoes, moving them aside to create space in the centre of the roasting tin, and cook everything for a further 10 minutes.

By now, the tomatoes and shallots will be golden and beginning to caramelise, and the goat's cheese will be soft and just beginning to run at the edges. Lightly toast the slices of sourdough bread (the pre-sliced Pain d'Alsace that we sell is perfect for this).

Cover each slice of toast with a couple of heaped tablespoons of the tomato mix. Top with 3-4 slices of the baked Golden Cross and garnish with a few fresh rosemary and basil leaves.

Celebrating the SEASONS

The Parsons Table is driven by a passion for true flavours, classic culinary techniques and seasonal ingredients.

Owners Lee and Liz Parsons opened The Parsons Table in December 2015 to much acclaim, but their culinary story began 20 years before that, when they first met working at Claridge's Hotel in London. From sous chef at Claridge's, where he worked for eight years, Lee went on to refine his cooking style under Raymond Blanc at Le Manoir aux Quat' Saisons.

This classic French training has influenced the way Lee prepares the locally sourced and seasonal ingredients at The Parsons Table – the tell-tale signs of his training can be seen in every beautiful sauce he makes.

From London, Lee and Liz moved to Canada, where Lee's successful career saw him become a regular on Canadian television. When Liz and Lee decided to move back to the UK with their twin girls, they decided it was time to open their very own restaurant – a lifelong ambition for Lee. Travelling between Liz's family in East Sussex and Lee's in Wiltshire, they often drove past the turrets and spires of Arundel – a pretty little town that would become the perfect home for their new restaurant.

The aim for this family-run restaurant was to create a place that they themselves would want to visit. It was about providing the utmost in quality and service, but, as Lee describes it, "stripping away the formalities of fine dining". Everything is made from scratch, including every stock and sauce, and they utilise the bounty of the surrounding area where they can.

The Parsons Table is becoming renowned for its fresh fish dishes thanks to its proximity to the sea. The catch of the day (which is sourced from Browns in Littlehampton) is often a local fish, and it is one of the areas where Lee loves to showcase his creativity. Above all, seasonality inspires Lee, taking simple ingredients and making them sing on the plate. He believes incredible locally sourced products make cooking more enjoyable and great ingredients equal great food.

Thanks to her many years in hotel management and event planning, Liz manages front of house. Attentive yet subtle service is what she strives for, and this goes hand-in-hand with the relaxed ambience of this popular Arundel restaurant.

The Parsons Table

LOIN OF SCOTT FREE-RANGE PORK, HAM HOCK CROQUETTE, SUMMER VEGETABLES, GOOSEBERRIES & MADEIRA SAUCE

Scott free-range, based on the outskirts of Storrington in West Sussex, produce first class pork from traditional breeds. The vegetables and gooseberries in this dish can easily be changed as the seasons move on.

Preparation time: 1 hour, plus 2 hours chilling | Cooking time: 5 hours | Serves 4

Ingredients

For the ham hock croquettes:

1 ham hock
1 carrot
1 celery stick
75g onion
1 bay leaf
2 fresh thyme sprigs
10g Italian parsley, chopped
15g aged Cheddar, grated
50g mayonnaise
½ tsp English mustard
½ tsp Dijon mustard
50g onion, finely chopped and blanched
20g flour
1 egg, beaten
30g white breadcrumbs
Salt and pepper

For the summer vegetables:

100g fresh peas
200g broad beans
8 baby carrots
1 small courgette
6 radishes (Easter egg or breakfast)
8 Jersey Royals
1 gem lettuce

For the Madeira sauce:

100g pork trimmings
50g shallots
50g black field mushrooms, chopped
30ml Sherry vinegar
500ml brown chicken stock
20ml double cream
150g Madeira, boiled
100ml Port, boiled
1 fresh thyme sprig
10 gooseberries, halved
Butter, for cooking

For the pork:

4 x 160g pork loin steaks

Method

For the ham hock croquettes

Wash the ham hock thoroughly. Place in a large pan, cover with cold water and bring to the boil. Drain. Cover the hock with cold water and repeat. Place the blanched ham hock back into the pan. Cover with cold water and bring to the boil. Simmer for 2 hours.

Peel and coarsely chop the carrot, celery and onion. Add to the simmering ham hock along with the bay leaf and thyme. Simmer for a further 2 hours or until the meat is falling from the bone. Remove from the heat and let it cool in the cooking liquor. Once cool, remove the hock from the cooking liquor. Finely shred the meat, removing excess fat and the skin. Place the shredded ham hock into a bowl. Add the parsley, Cheddar, mayonnaise and mustards along with the blanched onions. Season to taste. Shape into even balls and chill in the fridge for 2 hours. Once chilled and firm, flour, egg wash and breadcrumb the croquettes. Return to the fridge until required.

For the summer vegetables

Pod the peas and broad beans. Wash and peel the baby carrots. Slice the courgette into 3mm thick discs. Cut the radishes in half. Remove the outer leaves from the lettuce and wash. Wash the potatoes. Cook all of the above vegetables separately in boiling salted water until al dente.

For the Madeira sauce

Roast the pork trim in butter until caramelised. Add the shallots and mushrooms and cook for 4-5 minutes until golden. Add the vinegar and boil for 10 seconds. Add the remaining ingredients except the gooseberries. Bring to the boil, skim and simmer for 40 minutes. Strain through a fine sieve. Bring to the boil, skim the fat and then reduce to the correct consistency. Season to taste.

Warm the gooseberries in the sauce prior to serving.

For the pork and to serve

Preheat the oven to 180°c. Pan sear the pork until a deep golden colour all over (both sides and edges). Season to taste. Place onto a tray and cook in the preheated oven for 8-10 minutes. Sauté the cooked potatoes in a little butter until golden. Place into the oven for 5 minutes. Place the pork on to a cooling rack over a tray and allow to rest for 4-5 minutes. Deep-fry the ham croquette at 170°c until golden. Add the halved gooseberries to the sauce to warm. Reheat the blanched vegetables and season to taste. Place the lettuce leaves onto the plate, spoon the summer vegetables and potatoes around. Slice the pork in two. Add to the plate along with the croquette. Spoon the sauce and warmed gooseberries on to the plate, and serve.

Keeping it REAL

From one small bakery nearly 20 years ago to a collection of five flourishing individual shops across Brighton and Hove, Real Patisserie bakes fresh artisan bread, authentic patisseries and all manner of other delicious baked goods...

The very first Real Patisserie shop opened to the public in 1998, when Alastair Gourlay aimed to bring authentic patisserie and real bread to the people of Brighton. After just two years, the demand for the artisan products at his little Trafalgar Street shop had increased so much that Alastair opened a wholesale bakery near London Road.

A stream of further Real Patisserie shops then opened: Western Road, Hove in 2005; Kemptown in 2010; Shoreham in 2012; the Open Market, London Road in 2014; and, finally, Church Road, Hove in 2017. Each shop has a unique identity, its own individual character, and each one tells part of the Real Patisserie story.

The Western Road premises was the first open-plan bakery that enabled customers to watch savoury chefs and patissiers at work. This format has since become elemental in all Real Patisserie shops. The Kemptown shop, opened by Justin Gourlay, was the first to allow customers to see artisan bread being baked from scratch on the premises. The Shoreham store was opened with patissiers David and Helene Berthillot, is similarly open-planned and boasts an enviable location overlooking the harbour.

A medley of successful partnerships has allowed the shops to flourish, and the creativity of recipes and quality of food to continually develop, as ideas are passed from shop to shop.

This dynamic setup has ensured the success of these independently creative bakeries that are self-sufficient yet part of a wider brand. From cakes, tarts and patisserie to bread and savoury goods, everything is freshly made each day – much of it in full view of the customers. The Real Patisserie family are all passionate about letting people see exactly what they make and how they make it.

Real Patisserie
TARTE FLAMBEE

Any strong flour will work in this recipe, but traditional French baguette flour works best. You could also use ciabatta or pizza flour. It's convenient (and gives best results) if you mix the dough the day before and refrigerate overnight. If you need it for that day, that's fine, but you need to start preparing the dough 2 hours before using it.

Preparation time: 30 minutes, plus 2 hours proving | Cooking time: 10 minutes | Serves 6

Ingredients

For the dough:

500g bread flour

340ml water

5g fresh yeast (or 3g dried yeast), if preparing day before

10g fresh yeast (or 5g dried yeast), if preparing on the day

10g salt

Semolina flour for dusting (or you can use normal bread flour)

For the Moroccan lamb sauce:

300g lean lamb mince

½ onion

50g red and green pepper

2 garlic cloves, crushed

1 tsp chilli flakes

1 tsp ground cumin

½ tsp ground cinnamon

2 tbsp tomato purée

20g mint leaves

20g parsley leaves

For the salad:

200g golden beetroot, grated

200g crimson beetroot, grated

25ml olive oil

25ml balsamic vinegar

10ml honey

100g cherry tomatoes

Salt and pepper

To serve:

150g goat's curd, sour cream or crème fraîche

Method

For the dough

With one hand, mix the flour, water and yeast in a bowl and combine (keeping one hand clean is a very good idea!) Once the yeast is hidden in the mix, pour it out onto a surface and add the salt. Knead the dough for 5 minutes until there are no lumps and the dough is stretchy. This dough is quite wet, so won't form into a neat ball straight away. When you've finished kneading, throw some flour over it – the dough will then become much more manageable. Put the dough into a rectangular glass casserole dish or similar sized Tupperware, and either refrigerate overnight or put aside to prove at room temperature for 2 hours.

For the Moroccan lamb sauce

Put all the ingredients apart from the lamb into a food processor and pulse it until finely chopped but not a paste. Add the chopped ingredients to the minced lamb and combine. Add water until the mix is loose enough to spread easily with your fingers. Put in the fridge.

For the salad

Shake the olive oil, balsamic and honey in a jar until emulsified. Then combine the beetroots, tomatoes and dressing, and season with salt and pepper.

To assemble and serve

An hour before you want to eat, pour the dough out of your container, dusting with semolina and using a scraper or spatula to work the flour between the dough and the bowl to loosen it. Flatten it out roughly with your hands, and then roll with a rolling pin into a large rectangle about 5mm thick. If the dough won't stretch easily, rest it between rolls to allow it to loosen. Use as much flour as needed to prevent the dough sticking, but try not to drown it in flour.

Preheat your oven to 260°c/230°c fan. Arrange the wire shelves near the top and a baking tray on the floor of the oven.

Cut the dough into six pieces and arrange onto two parchment paper sheets; three on each piece. Spread each piece with the lamb sauce. When the oven is hot, place the parchment sheets into the oven, throw half a cup of water on the bottom tray to generate some steam and shut the door quickly. Bake for 10 minutes or to the required colour. Remove from the oven, cover with the salad and top with goat's curd, sour cream or crème fraîche. Eat open or fold over to enjoy as a sandwich.

Real Patisserie

BEETROOT, GOAT'S CHEESE, ROASTED GARLIC AND HAZELNUT QUICHE

This is one of the signature quiches at Real Patisserie – beautiful shortcrust pastry filled with a delicious, flavour-packed filling.

Preparation time: 30 minutes, plus 30 minutes chilling | Cooking time: 1½ hours | Serves 6

Ingredients

For the base:

200g flour

115g soft unsalted butter

1 egg

Pinch of salt

40ml cold water

For the egg mixture:

150ml cream

150ml whole milk

2 eggs

2 egg yolks

Large pinch of salt

For the filling:

1 whole bulb of garlic

200g cooked beetroot, cut into chunks

200g butternut squash, cut into chunks and blanched

50g cooked onion, sliced or diced

40g Cheddar cheese, grated

65g goat's cheese, crumbled or sliced

10 skinned hazelnuts, crushed

Pinch of dried rosemary

Pumpkin seeds, to decorate

Method

For the base

Grease a 23cm quiche or flan tin. Combine the flour, butter, egg and salt in a bowl, and mix into an even crumble with your fingertips. Add the cold water slowly, and work the mixture into a pastry. Do not overwork; once it has come together, wrap it in cling film and put in the fridge to chill for half an hour. Meanwhile, preheat the oven to 140°c (fan).

Take the pastry from the fridge and roll it into a sheet about 3mm thick. Drop the pastry loosely into the greased tin and work into the corners with your knuckles. Roll a rolling pin across the top to remove the excess pastry. Line the pastry with parchment and fill with baking beans, or rice if you don't have any beans. Bake for 40 minutes. At the same time bake the bulb of garlic. After taking out the pastry turn up the oven to 180°c and continue baking the garlic until it goes soft. Peel when cool.

For the egg mixture

Whisk all the ingredients together.

For the filling

Reduce the oven to 130°c. Mix the beetroot, butternut squash, onion and Cheddar cheese loosely together and put into the cooked quiche case.

Fill with the egg mixture, leaving a little room for decoration, about 1cm from the top.

Decorate the top of the quiche with the goat's cheese, hazelnuts, peeled garlic, rosemary and pumpkin seeds. Bake at 130°c for 45 minutes until the top of the quiche is firm to the touch with a little wobble.

Real Patisserie
CHOCOLATE
AND PISTACHIO DELIGHTS

To make this recipe perfectly you will need to be quite precise, so you will need electronic scales and a temperature probe. You will also need eight dome moulds to make these delights. If you've got too much mix prepared and not enough moulds, you can also serve in small glasses and/or freeze for another time. We recommend you make the biscuit, the cremeux and the mousse the day before so your portions have time to freeze overnight, and so you only have the glaze to pour on the day.

Preparation time: 24 hours | Cooking time: 15 minutes | Serves 8

Ingredients

For the gluten-free biscuit:

75g ground almonds

60g icing sugar

3 egg whites

30g whipping cream

20g dark chocolate chips, melted

1 tsp gluten-free flour

For the pistachio cremeux:

150g whipping cream

22g caster sugar

2 egg yolks

1g gelatine, softened in cold water

18g pistachio paste

For the milk chocolate mousse:

50g milk

50g whipping cream

20g egg yolks

10g caster sugar

110g milk chocolate chips

180g whipped cream

For the milk chocolate glaze:

60g water

120g glucose

120g caster sugar

80g condensed milk

9g gelatine, softened in 45g cold water

120g milk chocolate chips

To decorate:

A little dark chocolate for the tuiles

Finely chopped pistachios

Method

For the gluten-free biscuit

Preheat the oven to 160°c. Mix together the ground almonds, icing sugar and egg whites. Add the cream, melted dark chocolate chips, and gluten-free flour. Mix well and spread on to a baking tray, lined with parchment paper, to a depth of 1cm. Bake in the preheated oven for about 15 minutes. Allow to cool, then use a pastry cutter to cut into rounds the same size as the mould's base.

For the pistachio cremeux

Bring the cream to the boil. Mix the caster sugar and egg yolk together in a pan, then pour the cream over and bring the mix up to 82°c. Remove from the heat and add the softened gelatine. Finally add the pistachio paste. Place the cremeux in the fridge until set, then put into a piping bag and pipe into eight equal portions onto greaseproof paper, then freeze. These will form the centres of your pistachio delights.

For the milk chocolate mousse

Bring the milk and cream to the boil. Mix the egg yolks and caster sugar together. Add to the milk and cream. Bring the mixture up to 82°c. Remove from the heat and pour onto the milk chocolate chips and combine. Finally, gently mix in the whipped cream. Use a piping bag to half-fill the eight individual dome moulds with the mousse. Put one frozen pistachio cremeux in each, and cover with the rest of the chocolate mousse. Finish with the gluten-free biscuit. Freeze.

For the milk chocolate glaze

Bring the water, glucose and caster sugar to the boil. Remove from the heat and add the condensed milk then the softened gelatine and water. Bring to the boil, then remove from the heat. Add the milk chocolate chips and whisk until perfectly melted. Allow to cool to 40°c. Meanwhile, remove the frozen cakes from the moulds. Pour the milk chocolate glaze on to the frozen cakes. If the mixture is quite runny, you can do two coats, but leave a minute between each coat.

To decorate and serve

To decorate, make a thin chocolate tuile by melting a bit of dark chocolate, spreading it onto some greaseproof paper in a very thin layer, and cutting it with a warm pastry cutter. Keep the delights in the fridge until ready to serve. Decorate with the chocolate tuiles and some finely chopped pistachios. Delicious served with a scoop of ice cream and a red fruit salad.

Social DINING

A quirky tapas bar on up-and-coming London Road, Señor Buddha takes authentic Spanish tapas and adds a little twist of East Asian flavour.

Señor Buddha is owned and run by Lee Shipley, a self-taught chef with an enduring passion for the simplicity of the Spanish way of sharing small plates. Combined with his love of Asian flavours, Lee's enthusiasm for good food inspired him to put his unique stamp on the dining scene of Brighton.

The story began in the stunning island of Ibiza, where Lee fell in love with the pivotal role food plays in the daily lives of people. Gathering round tables with friends and family to share beautiful plates of freshly cooked food, the people here inspired Lee to try to recreate this atmosphere back in the UK.

Señor Buddha began life as a series of pop-ups, which Lee ran for around 18 months. The food was inspired by authentic dishes from every corner of Spain, but with Lee's own little twist – taking some bold and aromatic flavours from East Asia.

When it was time for Señor Buddha to move into a permanent home, the up-and-coming area of London Road seemed like the perfect option. This vibrant and quirky community was the ideal spot to open a bustling tapas bar.

Lee was in charge of the cooking at first, although today he has handed the reins to a head chef. He still enjoys having lots of input on the creative menu, which changes daily. For this reason, the menu is written on a blackboard each day, and Lee also shares it on social media to give diners a chance to see what each day's offerings will be.

The eclectic and interesting drinks menu takes inspiration from around the world and reflects the ever-changing menu. Along with Spanish wines you will find rum from the Philippines, gin from California, vodka from Russia and whisky from Japan.

The food and drink plays a huge part in the success of this award-winning tapas bar, but for Lee, one of the most important things is the culture that surrounds the sharing of these small plates. People come together to share tables, share food and enjoy the bustling energy of authentic Spanish dining.

Senor Buddha

PULPO WITH SOBRASSADA AND FENNEL PURÉE, SQUID INK SHARD AND CORIANDER AIOLI

Octopus is my favourite ingredient and it's rarely on British menus, but when it is done properly it's simply amazing. In this dish, we use a raw cured sausage from Ibiza and Majorca called Sobrassada. This dish takes a little forward planning but is a knock out for a dinner party.

Preparation time: 1 hour 10 minutes, plus 4-6 dehydrating | Cooking time: 2 hours 30 minutes | Serves 4

Ingredients

For the squid ink shard:

50ml Pedro Ximenez Jerez

75ml water

1 shallot, chopped

1 bunch coriander stalks (reserve the leaves for the coriander aioli)

5 garlic cloves, crushed

50g tapioca pearls

2 tbsp squid ink

For the octopus:

1.5-2kg octopus, defrosted and beak removed

For the sobrassada purée:

2 fennel bulbs

Oil, to drizzle

Sugar, to sprinkle

100-150g sobrassada

For the coriander aioli:

1 bunch of coriander, plus the extra leaves reserved from the squid ink shard

1 bunch of Thai basil

4 cloves garlic

1 shallot, chopped

110ml olive oil

1 lime, juiced

Salt, to taste

Method

For the squid ink shard

The night before you want to serve the dish, make the squid ink shard. Mix the first five ingredients together and heat to a rolling simmer, then leave to infuse for 1 hour. Strain the stock into a pan and bring the liquid to the boil. Add the tapioca pearls and simmer until all the pearls are soft. Drain if there any liquid is left, then return to the pan and stir in the squid ink; you need the mixture jet black so add more ink if you feel it needs more. Spread the pearls out on baking paper to form a flat sheet and dehydrate in a dehydrator at 65°c for 4-6 hours (if you don't have a dehydrator you can use your oven).

For the octopus

To cook the octopus, fill a large stock pot with salty water and bring to the boil. Dip the octopus in and out three or four times to stop the tentacles curling, then reduce to a rolling simmer and cook until tender; 60-90 minutes. A good way to see if it is tender is to stick a toothpick through a tentacle. When cooked, remove from the water and allow to cool. Cut off the tentacles by simply following the natural line of each tentacle to cut a v shape at the top of each tentacle.

For the sobrassada purée

Preheat the oven to 200°c. Halve the fennel bulbs and drizzle with oil and a sprinkle of sugar. Roast until soft, then place in a blender with 100g of sobrassada and blend. If the purée is wet, add more sobrassada; if it's too dry, add some of the cooking liquid from the roasted fennel until you have a spreadable and smooth consistency.

For the coriander aioli

Add the coriander, basil, garlic, shallots and 55ml of the oil to a blender and blend. Pour into a pot and add the other 55ml of oil and the lime juice. Stir together and add salt to taste.

To plate

Heat a griddle pan or frying pan on high heat, oil the octopus tentacles and cook until charred and heated through. Run a line of sobrassada purée down the centre of the plate, run two smaller lines of coriander aioli either side of the purée, then place two tentacles on the sobrassada purée. Balance the squid ink shard against the tentacle.

Enjoy with a large glass of Verdejo.

All about the
HOUMOUS

Made from a recipe that has taken 25 years to perfect, it is no surprise that Smorl's Houmous is now Brighton's best-loved homemade houmous.

Smorl's Houmous, Falafel and Salad Bar is an independent market café run by foodie siblings Sarah (also known as Smorl) and Christian (or Xian). It all started with Sarah's famous houmous, the recipe for which she has been perfecting for a quarter of a century.

Her passion for houmous began 25 years ago when working with an Israeli friend making houmous and falafel in a tent at Glastonbury. She fell in love with Middle Eastern food and has been developing her own houmous recipe ever since. In 2000, Sarah began selling her dip at markets and food festivals. It soon got to the point where Sarah's home kitchen couldn't sustain the demand for her houmous… enter brother Christian.

Christian has worked for the much-loved Brighton vegetarian restaurant Terre a Terre since it opened in 1993, where he pursued his love of vegetarian cuisine for over 20 years, managing front of house first, followed by operations. In 2014, he combined his restaurant expertise with his sister's houmous business to create Smorl's Ltd. They set about expanding their wholesale production and opened Smorl's Houmous, Falafel and Salad Bar in the new London Road Open Market.

Alongside Smorl's legendary houmous, the café sells freshly fried falafel, freshly baked pitta pockets, salad boxes, mezze cake, soups, house-recipe deli pots and many other delicious things. Everything is strictly vegetarian (including cheeses) and there are plenty of vegan and gluten-free options, too. The only things not made in house are the fluffy pittas, which are delivered each day from an Israeli baker.

However, despite the mouth-watering array of brunch and lunch options, the vegan and gluten-free houmous is still the star of the show at Smorl's. Made from organic chickpeas and locally sourced ingredients where possible, it currently comes in four varieties: Original, Fresh Chilli, Extra Garlic and Thunder Garlic. The chickpeas are cooked with organic Cornish kombu seaweed to aid digestion and add a unique 'umami' flavour. From the hand-peeled garlic and hand-squeezed lemon juice to the premium tahini and extra-virgin olive oil, they don't cut any corners and never compromise on quality.

Smorl's

Smorl's
SAVOURY VEGAN MEZZE CAKE

There are lots of elements to this impressive dish. You will need a 20cm sturdy spring-form circular cake tin, well oiled.

Preparation time: 1 hour | Cooking time: 4 hours | Serves 6-8

Ingredients

For the falafel mix:

200g dried chickpeas

60g flat leaf parsley, stalks removed

50g red onion, finely chopped

2 cloves garlic, minced

1 heaped tsp salt

1½ tsp ground cumin

1 tbsp ground coriander

¼ tsp cayenne pepper

¼ tsp smoked paprika

For the aubergine purée:

1 large aubergine

20g sun-dried tomatoes

Sprig of fresh rosemary

Large pinch of Maldon salt flakes

Glug of olive oil

For the butternut squash purée:

1 large butternut squash

Pinch of salt

Glug of olive oil

¼ tsp ground cinnamon

½ tbsp date syrup

½ tbsp tahini

For the spicy tomato bulgur wheat:

50ml sunflower oil

½ tsp fennel seeds

½ tsp cumin seeds

100g red onion, finely chopped

80g tomato purée

1 can chopped tomatoes

1 stock cube (vegan)

20ml olive oil

200g bulgur wheat

1 tsp Maldon salt

½ tsp cayenne pepper

¼ tsp smoked paprika

¼ tsp ground cinnamon

½ tsp ground cloves

For the sun-blush tomato and beetroot purée:

100g raw beetroot, grated

100g carrot, grated

80g sun-blush tomatoes (in oil), drained

1 capful (or to taste) chilli sauce

To assemble:

4 fresh pitta breads

200g Smorl's Original Houmous (or Extra Garlic, or Thunder Garlic, if you dare)

Olive oil, to drizzle

Method

For the falafel mix

Soak the chickpeas for 12 hours in 1 litre of water. Drain and rinse the chickpeas, then grind through a meat grinder or Kenwood attachment with the parsley, onion and garlic. Add the salt and spices, and mix well.

For the aubergine purée

Preheat oven to 180°c. Cut the aubergine almost in half and stuff it with the other ingredients. Wrap tightly in foil and roast for 1½ hours until soft. Discard the stalk and rosemary. Liquidise the remainder into a purée.

For the butternut squash purée and discs

While the aubergine is roasting, peel the squash and chop in half, separating the 'top' half from the 'bulbous' half. Cut the 'bulbous' end in half and remove the seeds. Chop the flesh roughly and mix with salt, olive oil and cinnamon. Roast in the oven at 180°c with the aubergine, covered with foil for 40 minutes. Meanwhile, slice the 'top' half of squash into thin discs, arrange on an oven dish, sprinkle with salt and olive oil, cover in foil and bake for around 15 minutes. Remove from the oven while still firm. Remove the 'bulbous' mix from oven, stir in the date syrup, and liquidise the mixture, adding the tahini to produce a thick purée.

For the spicy tomato bulgur wheat

Heat the sunflower oil in a heavy saucepan, add the fennel and cumin seeds, and fry for 1 minute. Add the onion, stir, cover and sweat on a low heat for 10 minutes. Add the tomato purée and fry gently for a few minutes, stirring. Stir in the canned tomatoes and stock cube. Add ½ can of water, stir in and leave to simmer on low heat. Add the olive oil to a second pan on low heat. Add the bulgur wheat and salt, and stir regularly for 10 minutes. Add the spices, stirring rapidly. Add the tomato sauce, mix thoroughly and cover. Return to a low heat for 5 minutes, then let cool for 30 minutes.

For the sun-blush tomato and beetroot purée

Blitz all the ingredients together with a stick blender.

To assemble

Split the pittas lengthways to produce 8 thin circular breads. Soak the four thickest pieces briefly in water. Line the bottom of an oiled 20cm cake tin with the wet pittas (cut into shapes to allow even coverage). Spread half the houmous over evenly. Spread 300g of the falafel mix on top. Cover with 200g aubergine purée. Layer the squash discs on top and spread 200g butternut purée evenly on top. Sprinkle the bulgur wheat mixture as the next layer and press down. Cover with 280g beetroot purée. Use the remaining pitta halves to cover the top, cutting into shapes for even coverage. Top with the remaining houmous. Cover with cling film and weigh down. Place in the fridge for at least 30 minutes. Preheat the oven to 210°c.

Remove the cling film and drizzle a little olive oil over the top. Cover lightly with foil and bake for 80 minutes. Uncover the cake, reduce to 180°c and cook for a further 40 minutes, but remove early if the top is 'catching'. Leave to cool before removing from the tin. You can decorate with houmous piping – try Smorl's Chilli Houmous or create a piping mix with liquidised canned chickpeas with natural colourings and flavourings.

Shop LOCAL

An award-winning food shop and café, The Sussex Produce Company boasts the county's largest range of locally made products all under one roof.

Owner of The Sussex Produce Company, Nick Hempleman, is passionate about the produce of his home county. He was born and spent his childhood in Steyning, and decided to open the shop to showcase the bounty of the area he grew up in.

The Sussex Produce Company opened in November 2007 with two main aims: to champion the best Sussex farmers and producers; and to establish a business that invests in its local economy and infrastructure.

In 2017, 10 years since it first opened its doors, the shop now features 205 suppliers, of which 170 are based in Sussex. This impressive list makes The Sussex Produce Company the largest stockist of local produce in the county.

The shop was joined by an on-site café when they moved to larger premises in 2011 and the two branches of the business, sitting side-by-side, create an irresistible buzz of activity. The café acts as a showcase for the products sold in the shop – what better way to try some of them or get inspiration for cooking ideas?

Everything is cooked from scratch, from homemade breakfasts to seasonal lunches, and on Sundays the café serves up a delicious roast. It's understandably popular, though, so it's advised to book ahead. For those with a sweet tooth, artisan cakes can be enjoyed alongside tea and freshly ground coffee.

On Friday and Saturday evenings the atmosphere changes. The bustle of the shop disappears, the lights are replaced with flickering candles and customers can enjoy seasonal evening meals freshly prepared by the chefs. A drinks list is available, but many diners like to choose a bottle from the shop to drink with their meal for a small corkage charge.

Named as one of the best independent retailers in the South from The Observer Food Monthly Awards, and twice named Sussex food shop of the year at the Sussex Food & Drink Awards, The Sussex Produce Company has also been a winner at the Farm Shop & Deli Awards and the Sussex Countryside Trust Awards.

And with high-profile praise from culinary stars Mary Berry and Prue Leith, it's no surprise this Steyning gem has become a cherished part of the West Sussex food scene.

We are much more than
Beautiful, Fresh, Local
Produce....
Please Come in for a
Browse!

Sussex Produce Company

eafy Carrot Bunch
ourgette

Sussex
Savoy Cabbage
Local Parsnips

Beetroot Bu
Local Red Ca

LOCAL GRILLED SEA BASS WITH A SAMPHIRE AND ASPARAGUS SAUTÉED SALAD, AND BROWN SHRIMP AND HERB BUTTER

The flavour of fresh local sea bass is elevated in this simple dish thanks to the buttery shrimps, asparagus and samphire, and the lemony crushed potatoes.

Preparation time: 15 minutes | Cooking time: 30 minutes | Serves 6

Ingredients

700g new potatoes

12 local sea bass fillets (I work on 2 fillets per person. You can ask any good fishmonger to prep the fillets for you. Just ask for scaled, pinned and trimmed.)

225g butter

1 lemon, juiced

500g samphire (pick off the woody stems)

2 bunches asparagus, shaved (you can use your vegetable peeler)

200 brown shrimps

1 bunch of dill, finely chopped

1 bunch of parsley, finely chopped

1 bunch of chives, finely chopped

Salt

Vegetable oil, for frying

Method

Boil the new potatoes in salted water then put to one side and keep warm.

Season the sea bass with salt and pepper whilst heating up a frying pan. Fry the sea bass in vegetable oil skin-side down. When the sea bass is half-cooked, turn it over, adding some of the butter and half of the lemon juice to the pan, then remove from the heat. Leave for 2 minutes and then remove the sea bass from the pan, returning the pan to the heat.

Once the pan is hot again, add the samphire and asparagus. Once cooked, add the brown shrimps, half of the remaining butter, and half of the chopped herbs. Stir.

Pour the remaining lemon juice over the new potatoes, adding the remaining herbs and butter. Use a fork to crush this all together.

Serve the sea bass with the samphire, asparagus, shrimp and crushed potatoes.

Uniquely SUSSEX

SussexFood offer sensational catering for the bespoke eateries, coffee shops and conference facilities at the University of Sussex's beautiful campus in Falmer.

Set within the idyllic landscape of the Sussex Downs, The University of Sussex is a thriving higher education establishment that is home to over 16,000 students and 2,000 members of staff – not to mention numerous visitors to the site. SussexFood takes pride in catering for these thousands of people each day with a whole host of unique eateries.

Six cafés, two restaurants, a lively café bar attached to the university's theatre, a street food van and an array of pop-ups – SussexFood has got every dining option covered. Each venue has its own identity, but what unites them all is the focus on nutritious, locally sourced food. What's on offer includes Eat Central, which serves globally inspired food from breakfast through to dinner, The Dhaba Cafe, which specialises in vegan and vegetarian dishes, and Arts Piazza, which is a coffee-lovers dream thanks to its triple-certified coffee and first-rate baristas.

Although each eatery has a totally unique atmosphere and personality of its own, all the venues are united by their contemporary menus that keep up with Brighton's trendy reputation, as well as their ethical approach to sourcing ingredients.

This ethos continues with the conference and event services at The University of Sussex. Under the brand Space with US, the conference menus support local growers by using the very best and freshest produce from the region. These ingredients are then transformed into creative dishes by a team of talented chefs who can create menus for anything from breakfasts and buffet lunches to canapes and afternoon cakes.

The onsite conference centre is not only a favourite with university departments, but also attracts many external clients. From national corporations hosting huge events to smaller local businesses staging training days, the Space with US team can offer competitively priced packages to suit any occasion – all within the university's many buildings and state-of-the-art conference centre.

"MAC" & "CHEESE"

TREACLE-GLAZED SUSSEX PORK

Space with US cater for high-end conferences and events,
here is an example of just one of the delicious dishes on offer.

Preparation time: 30 minutes | Cooking time: 3 hours | Serves 6

Ingredients

For the pork belly:

1kg belly pork joint from a local butcher (ask to take out any bones)

Oil, for rubbing

Salt

For the Scotch eggs:

3 boiled eggs, cooled and peeled

180g Sussex sausage meat from a local butcher

¼ teaspoon mustard powder

A pinch of freshly grated nutmeg

A pinch of cayenne pepper

200g panko breadcrumbs (or normal breadcrumbs if not available)

100g plain flour

2 eggs, beaten

Oil, for deep-frying

For the pork fillet:

500g pork fillet, trimmed of sinew & fat, marinated in 100g black treacle

100g black pudding, diced

Oil and butter, for cooking

To serve:

200g baby heritage carrots, scraped and blanched

200g baby coloured beetroot, cooked, peeled and halved

100g petit pois, blanched

½ head baby gem lettuce, shredded

100g salted butter

500g mashed potatoes, preferably Maris Piper

100ml double cream

Micro cress or other herbs, to garnish

200ml beef jus or gravy

Oil and butter, for cooking

Salt and pepper

Method

For the pork belly

Preheat the oven to 180°c/fan 160°c. Lay the pork belly, skin-side up, on a rack in a roasting tin. Rub with oil and scatter with salt to help the fat run out and the skin to crisp. Cook in the oven for 2 hours 15 minutes, then increase the heat to 200°c (fan 180°c) for 35 minutes to crisp the crackling. Once tender, leave to rest for 10-15 minutes.

For the Scotch eggs

Pour 1-2 inches of water into a saucepan then bring to the boil. Place the eggs into the saucepan, cover with a lid, reduce the heat to medium-high and cook until the yolks are soft; about 4½ minutes. Remove from the pan and cover with cold water to halt the cooking. Once cool, peel and dry on paper towels.

Mix the sausage, mustard, nutmeg and cayenne and shape into six balls. Lay a piece of cling film on a flat surface. Place one ball of sausage mixture into the centre of the cling film, fold the cling film over and flatten into an ⅛ inch thick oval. Pull the cling film back and place an egg in the centre. Press the sausage around the egg to cover. Repeat with remaining eggs and sausage. Store in the refrigerator.

Place the breadcrumbs in one shallow bowl, the flour in another and the beaten eggs in a third. Roll the eggs in flour, then egg, then breadcrumbs. Allow any excess breadcrumbs to fall away. Set aside.

For the pork fillet

Preheat the oven to 180°c (fan 160°c). Wipe any excess treacle from the pork. Heat a little oil in a hot pan then add the fillet. Turn down the heat slightly and seal on all sides. Add some butter and gently coat the pork with the foaming butter and oil for a couple of minutes over the heat. Add the diced black pudding and transfer to the hot oven for 3 minutes or until cooked to your liking. Allow to rest on a wire rack.

Back to the Scotch eggs

Heat the oil for deep-frying. Working in batches, cook the eggs in the preheated oil until golden; 5-6 minutes. Transfer to a wire rack to cool; at least 5 minutes.

To serve

Heat a frying pan with some oil and a little butter. Add the carrots and beetroot, gently warm through and season. Remove and keep warm. In same pan, heat the petits pois, then, once warm, add the shredded lettuce, season and remove from the heat. Heat a second frying pan and add the butter. Once melted, add the mashed potatoes and heat through. Add the cream to the required consistency, which should be just firm enough to peak and able to be piped. Adjust the seasoning.

Take the crackling off the pork belly and cut up. Slice the belly into six pieces. Cut the pork fillet into six discs. Cut the Scotch eggs in half. On the plate, pipe two swirls of mashed potatoes, place the pork belly at one end of the plate, pork fillet in the middle and half a Scotch egg at the other end. Arrange the carrots, beetroot, peas and lettuce around the centrepiece. Sprinkle crackling over the top of the dish, adding edible herbs or cress to garnish. Finish off with reduced jus or gravy.

Sussex FOOD HEROES

Family-run fishmongers Veasey & Sons has accumulated some impressive awards in its first seven years of business – and it has ambitious plans for the future, too.

It's hard to believe that Veasey & Sons has only been in business since 2010, especially considering the list of accolades they have gathered so far. Named The Best Food Shop in Sussex and Fishmonger of the Year, they were also finalists of BBC Radio 4's Food & Farming Awards (for Best Local Food Retailer) and Sussex Life Awards (for High Street Hero).

However, in 2009, life was very different for owners Chris and Dan. Dan was working as a chef, while Chris (his father-in-law) was a fisherman. As money was declining for fishermen, Chris was looking into ways he could sell his catch directly to customers. He began at East Grinstead farmers' market, and, following success there, he joined forces with chef Dan to open their own fishmongers in Forest Row.

Despite not being by the coast, this village fishmongers has certainly made waves. The family feel is evident as soon as you enter. Three generations of family currently work there (Chris, his wife Simone, his father John and son-in-law Dan). The team also includes Charlie, who does most of the cooking; Will, who is in charge of smoking the fish; and Nick, who is a familiar face in the shop and at markets.

Chris's fishing boat is still a special part of the business. What they don't fish themselves, they source from reputable suppliers with a focus on wild British fish. Depending on the time of year, the counter can contain huss, whiting, hake, line-caught sea bass, mackerel, gurnard, and they even catch their own cod in season – something that is a world away from the supermarket offerings.

As well as fresh fish, they also specialise in smoked fish, which they smoke in-house. Home-smoked cod, salmon and haddock is then used in their handmade patés. They are currently finalising their on-site production kitchen in order to expand the selection of prepared items. From fish pies and fishcakes to sauces and soups, they aim to be a one-stop-shop for fish. For those not living near Forest Row, Veasey & Sons can be found at a number of markets in Sussex, Kent, Surrey and London, find the details of your nearest market at www.veaseyandsons.co.uk/markets.

The whole team are passionate cooks and love to give cooking tips. Being part of the process every step of the way (the fishing, landing, weighing and grading, storage, preparation, smoking and cooking) means there is nothing they do not know about their products.

Veasey & Sons
THE CLASSIC FISHCAKE

The Veasey & Sons classic fishcake
has to be one of the most popular products we make.

Preparation time: 20 minutes | Cooking time: 20 minutes | Serves 6

Ingredients

500g Veasey & Sons mixed fish mix

350g naturally smoked haddock, skinned, boned and diced

500ml milk

1 bay leaf

1kg Maris Piper potatoes, peeled and chopped

1 bunch spring onions, sliced

1 tsp Dijon mustard

1 tbsp mayonnaise

50g capers (drained), roughly chopped

50g cornichons (drained), roughly chopped

1 tbsp flat leaf parsley, finely chopped

1 tbsp chives, finely chopped

1 lemon, zested and juiced

Plain flour

3 eggs, beaten with a splash of milk

Panko breadcrumbs

Salt and pepper

Sunflower oil, for frying

Method

Place the fish into a deep frying pan, cover with milk, season and add the bay leaf. Cook for 5 minutes until the fish is flakey, then drain well and set aside.

Place the potatoes into a large saucepan, bring to the boil and simmer until tender. Drain and mash thoroughly, and season to taste. Mix the mashed potatoes with the spring onions, dijon mustard, mayonnaise, capers, cornichons, flat leaf parsley, chives, and lemon zest and juice, then carefully fold in the fish.

Prepare three deep dishes: put the plain flour in one; the beaten eggs with a splash of milk in the second; and the panko breadcrumbs in the third.

Divide the mixture into six portions and shape each into a thick fishcake. Roll each fishcake into the flour, then the egg and then the breadcrumbs.

Heat a large frying pan and add the oil to the pan to a depth of 1cm. Place the fish cakes into the pan and slowly fry until golden brown and hot in the middle. Serve with a dressed salad and a nice mayonnaise, enjoy!

Veasey & Sons
PAN-ROASTED SUSSEX COD WITH GARLIC LEMON MASH AND BUTTERED SAMPHIRE

The flavour of freshly caught Sussex cod is really something special, and it is lovely served alongside deliciously citrusy and garlicky mashed potatoes and some tasty buttered samphire.

Preparation time: 20 minutes | Cooking time: 20 minutes | Serves 4

Ingredients

800g Maris Piper potatoes, peeled and roughly chopped

4 garlic cloves, peeled

1 large lemon, zested and juiced

150g salted butter

100ml double cream

Plain flour, for coating

4 x 180g pieces of cod loin, skin on

2 tbsp sunflower oil

2 handfuls samphire, woody stalks removed (or trimmed fine beans)

16 cherry plum tomatoes, quartered

Salt and pepper

Method

Place the potatoes and the garlic cloves into a pan, cover with water and bring to the boil. Simmer until the potatoes are tender. Drain the potatoes well, mash thoroughly, season, and then add the lemon zest, 50g of the butter and the cream. Cover, set aside and keep warm.

Preheat the oven to 180°c. Season the plain flour with the salt and pepper, roll the cod loin in the flour and set aside.

Heat a large, thick-bottomed, metal-handled frying pan and add the oil. Fry the cod loins, skin-side down first, until golden in colour, finishing skin-side up. Place the pan into the oven for 5 minutes to finish them off.

Heat a deep frying pan, add 50g of the butter and the samphire. Toss in the pan until coated, then add the tomatoes and the remaining 50g of the butter, followed by the lemon juice.

Add a spoonful of mash onto each warmed plate, place the cod on top and divide the samphire mixture between the plates, drizzling the remainder of the lemon butter to dress the dish.

Natural PARTNERSHIP

A friendship between two Sussex businesses is creating a vision of sustainable farming around one of the world's oldest plants – Vitality Hemp meets Slake Spirits.

Taking ancient ingredients and crafts, and bringing them into the modern day is something both Slake Spirits and Vitality Hemp share. They plan to enter a joint venture together where they can start to sow the seeds of regenerative agriculture and environmentally-conscious business in Sussex. Working together will allow them to put their land ethics to the top of the agenda to create sustainable products in a truly organic way.

Nathaniel Loxley founded Vitality Hemp at the end of 2014, Enthused by not only the versatility of hemp but also by its staggering nutritional qualities, Nathaniel set about growing hemp naturally at the foot of the South Downs.

While attending a Prince's Trust event, Nathaniel met Tom Martin-Wells, trained chemist, budding botanist and owner of Slake Spirits, an independent gin distillery in Shoreham-by-Sea. Nathaniel and Tom shared many ideas and philosophies when it came to their goals and running their businesses – both being interested in Aldo Leopold's land ethic and how this philosophy could relate to companies' social and environmental impacts, seeing themselves as having a distinct relationship with the environment and a responsibility to look after the land on which they grow their crops and produce their products.

Taking the hemp from seed to shelf, Vitality Hemp celebrates the nutritional benefit of hemp in oil, protein powder and coffee, although Nathaniel admits there are endless uses for this special seed. It's a complete food source (in fact you could probably live on it alone) containing the perfect balance of omega oils, it is also a vegan source of digestible protein, fibre and the full range of essential amino acids.

Nathaniel is keen on taking this heritage ingredient and working with other like-minded producers to build the local economy and produce their own food and drink.

Tom at Slake Spirits shares this passion, crafting his locally produced spirits using hand-picked, wild, foraged botanicals alongside traditional flavours. His drinks are inspired by the natural world around him. From Slake HQ in his grandad's old woodwork hideaway, Tom combines nature with science in hand-crafting his small-batch gins.

You'll find them both at local farmer's markets, but you can also buy direct from their websites. An exciting partnership for the environment, it's also a perfect celebration of the bounty of Sussex's natural larder.

Photograph: Frankie Knight

Photograph: Frankie Knight

Vitality Hemp
HERITAGE TOMATO AND HEMP SALAD

You can source all of your hemp ingredients via www.vitalityhemp.com. Rocket and red mustard leaves can provide a similar flavour to the hemp leaves, but nothing beats the real thing!

Preparation time: 20 minutes | Cooking time: 12 minutes | Serves 4

Ingredients

For the roasted hemp seeds:

100g whole hemp seeds

1 tsp olive oil

Sea salt and black pepper

For the tomato salad:

400g mixed ripe tomatoes

1 handful black olives

1 glug balsamic vinegar

2 handfuls young hemp leaves

Sea salt

For the hemp seed oil pesto:

1 handful pine nuts

1 garlic clove

3 handfuls fresh basil leaves

1 handful grated Parmesan cheese (or 1 handful soaked and drained cashews with 2 tbsp nutritional yeast for a vegan alternative)

3–4 tbsp Vitality Hemp Seed Oil

½ lemon, juiced

Sea salt and black pepper

Method

For the toasted hemp seeds

Preheat the oven to 160°c. Place the whole hemp seeds in the oven to roast for 12 minutes (until they start to colour and crack). Empty the seeds into a bowl, add the olive oil and season generously with sea salt and black pepper. Mix well and leave to cool.

For the tomato salad

Roughly chop the tomatoes and olives, and mix together with a pinch of sea salt and a drizzle of balsamic vinegar.

For the hemp seed oil pesto

Dry roast the pine nuts in a pan. Pulse the garlic clove in a blender with a pinch of sea salt. Next add the basil leaves, pulse again. Add the pine nuts along with the Parmesan (or cashews and nutritional yeast). Blend whilst pouring the hemp seed oil and lemon juice through the funnel until you get the consistency you want.

To serve

Plate up the tomato mixture, adding a scattering of fresh, succulent hemp leaves. A generous drizzle of the pesto for each portion will leave you with ample leftover for another dish in the next few days, if it's refrigerated. Finish the dish off with a topping of toasted hemp seeds alongside crusty bread.

Slake Spirits
HEMP REVIVER

This cocktail was created by Sergio Kenkel at The Cocktail Shack, Brighton. Fresh hemp leaves have a delightful citrus aroma and flavour with a subtle bitterness; an ideal cocktail ingredient. Whilst more of a gin sour than a member of the, sadly, largely forgotten 'corpse reviver' family, the hemp reviver is all about bringing back this much maligned, but nutritious and delicious ingredient.

Syrup | Preparation time: 1 minute | Cooking time: 30 minutes | Serves 10-20
Cocktail | Preparation time: 5 minutes | Mixing time: 3 minutes | Serves 1 or more!

Ingredients

For the hemp syrup:

Large handful fresh Vitality Hemp hemp leaves

2 parts sugar or honey

1 part water

For the cocktail:

1 part hemp syrup (see above)

1½ parts Slake Spirits Sussex Dry gin

1 part fresh lime juice

1 part egg white

Ice

Orange twist and fresh hemp leaf, to garnish

Method

For the hemp syrup

Make this ahead of time and store in the fridge. Place the hemp leaves in a saucepan, cover with 2 parts sugar or honey and 1 part water. Simmer on a medium heat until the syrup is flavoured as you would like. Allow to cool and fine-strain into a sterilised jar or bottle. Once sealed, this should keep for at least a month.

For the cocktail

Take 1 part hemp syrup and add to a shaker with 1½ parts Slake Spirits Sussex Dry Gin. If necessary, gently stir with a bar spoon until dissolved. Add 1 part lime juice and 1 part egg white. Dry shake all the ingredients vigorously, but be careful to equalise the pressure (by carefully opening and then closing the shaker) after the first shake or two to avoid cocktail-covered walls! Add a generous scoop of ice and shake again to chill. Fine-strain and serve in a chilled coupe or martini glass. Garnish with an orange twist and hemp leaf. Enjoy!

The freshest CATCH

A family business through and through, Wolfies of Hove has been racking up the awards not only in Brighton but nationally, too...

Wolfies of Hove is run by Danny Keston, his father David, uncle Derek and little brother Jake – a family who all know a thing or two about fresh fish. They pride themselves on serving the best fish and chips in the Brighton and Hove area, but they actually have an award putting them in the top 10 fish and chip shops in the country. No mean feat!

So, what is it about Wolfies of Hove that makes their food so special? For Danny, it all comes down to sourcing the very best quality. They work with a local fisherman to get the best of the day's catch, as well as a local farm for their potatoes.

Alongside classic offerings, such as cod, Wolfies is known for its weekly specials, which can range from Jerk-battered red snapper to gin and tonic-battered scallops. They also work hard to showcase more unusual local fish, such as huss, which has a uniquely sweet taste thanks to its diet of spider crabs in the local waters. They are also famous for their smoked haddock and soft-shell crab, as well as their handmade fish cakes.

Wolfies is renowned for having lots to offer its gluten-free guests. In fact, the gluten-free batter and gluten-free sausages helped them bring home an award for best gluten-free fish and chip shop in the country.

The shop is named after a Jewish deli in the US, where the family once travelled. Each day they were mesmerised by its long queue snaking through the neighbourhood and were desperate to try it. When they decided to set up their own business, they decided to name it after this popular hotspot hoping a little bit of that charm would follow the name – and looking at the queues outside Wolfies of Hove, it certainly did!

The future for the Wolfies team is busy with a new café opening just a couple of doors away. Wolfies Kitchen is doing for breakfast and brunch what its big sister has done for fish and chips – using the finest and freshest ingredients to create the tastiest meals.

Wollies of Hove
HADDOCK & COD SCOTCH EGG

A delicious fish variation of a classic Scotch egg.

Preparation time: 30 minutes, plus 2-3 hours setting | Cooking time: 10 minutes | Serves 4

Ingredients

4 eggs, plus 2 egg whites

150g cod

60ml double cream

Pinch of salt

400ml milk

150g smoked haddock

Sprig of tarragon, chopped

½ lemon, juiced

Plain flour, for coating

Handful of breadcrumbs

Oil, for deep-frying

Tartare sauce, to serve

Rocket, to serve

Method

Boil the eggs in a pan of boiling water until just cooked – cook for 5 minutes for the yolks to stay runny. Place in iced water to stop them cooking any further.

Put the cod in a food processor and blitz. Add 1 egg white and blitz to a purée. Add the cream and a pinch of salt.

Put the milk and haddock in a pan. Heat until cooked through. Remove the haddock from the milk and flake it into small pieces. Leave to cool, then add to the cod purée. Add the chopped tarragon, lemon juice and season to taste.

Peel the eggs and dust each egg with plain flour, then coat with the fish mixture. Wrap in cling film and chill for 2-3 hours until set.

Put some plain flour in one bowl, the remaining egg white (whisked) in another bowl and the breadcrumbs in a third bowl. Coat each egg in the flour, then the egg, then the breadcrumbs.

Heat the oil for deep-frying in a small saucepan and deep-fry the eggs in the hot oil until golden.

Carefully lower each Scotch egg into the oil and cook for 5 minutes, or until golden brown. It's best to cook no more than two at a time. Remove with a slotted spoon and drain on kitchen paper. Leave to cool before serving.

Serve with tartare sauce and some fresh rocket.

The DIRECTORY

These great businesses have supported the making of this book; please support and enjoy them.

BeFries
46 West Street
Brighton BN1 2RA
Telephone: 01273 253570
Website: www.befries.com
Award-winning Belgian fries – double-cooked and saucy.

Bluebird Tea Co.
41 Gardner St
Brighton BN1 1UN
Telephone: 01273 325 523
Website: www.bluebirdteaco.com
Bluebird Tea Co. is a fairly young, independent, award-winning, unique Tea Mixology Company on a mission to make people happy with tea!

Bolney Wine Estate
Foxhole Lane
Bolney
West Sussex RH17 RNB
Telephone: 01444 881575
Website: www.bolneywineestate.com
Beautiful Sussex vineyard with café, cellar door, tours and trail, selling award-winning still and sparkling wines.

Edgcumbes Coffee Roasters & Tea Merchants
The Old Barn, Ford Lane
Arundel
West Sussex BN18 0DF
Telephone: 01243 555 775 (office/admin) 01243 519995 (café/shop)
Website: www.edgcumbes.co.uk
Coffee roasters and tea merchants with café and food academy.

Egg & Spoon
107-108 St George's Road
Brighton BN2 1EA
Telephone: 01273 603411
Website: www.eggandspoon.net
Neighbourhood café in Kemptown and innovative bespoke catering company.

etch. by Steven Edwards
216 Church Road
Brighton & Hove BN3 2DJ
Telephone: 01273 227485
Website: www.etchfood.co.uk
Steven Edwards' first restaurant, with menus focusing on fresh produce in and around the surrounding Sussex countryside.

Garlic Wood Farm
50 High Street
Steyning
West Sussex BN44 3RD
Telephone: 01903 812 685
Website: www.garlicwoodfarm.co.uk
Independent butchery specialising in rare-breed and native meat, offering butchery courses and event catering.

The Great British Charcuterie Co.
Unit 40 Brighton Marina
Brighton BN2 5WA
Telephone: 01273 695278
Website:
www.thegreatbritishcharcuterie.co.uk
Artisan British charcuterie, cheeses and English wines, alongside many more outstanding British products.

hiSbe
20-21 York Place
Brighton, BN1 4GU
Telephone: 01273 608 028
Website: www.hisbe.co.uk
hiSbe Food is a different kind of supermarket, on a mission to break the mould by putting customers, suppliers and employees first.

Isaac At

2 Gloucester Street,
Brighton BN1 4EW
Telephone: 07765934740
Website: www.isaac-at.com
Fine-dining restaurant with a key focus on locally sourced ingredients and an all-British drinks menu.

Marwood Bar & Coffeehouse

52 Ship Street
Brighton BN1 1AF
Telephone: 01273 382063
Website: www.themarwood.com
A place staffed by a bunch of coffee ninjas, just trying to get by, who hope one day to sell enough flat whites to buy a Greek island and spend the rest of our days drinking pina coladas.

Metrodeco

38 Upper St James's St,
Brighton BN21JN
Telephone: 01273677243
Website: www.metro-deco.com
We are a quirky vintage cafe that specialises in loose-leaf tea, afternoon tea and tea cocktails.

Pallant of Arundel

The Town Square
17 High Street
Arundel BN18 9AD
Telephone: 01903 882288
Website: www.pallantofarundel.co.uk
Purveyors of fine food and wine.

The Parsons Table

2 & 8 Tarrant Street
Arundel
West Sussex BN18 9DG
Telephone: 01903 883 477
Website: www.theparsonstable.co.uk
The Parsons Table showcases a deep passion for locally sourced, seasonal food, classic cooking and incredible flavours in an informal and relaxed environment.

Presuming Ed's Coffee House

114-115 London Road
Brighton BN1 4LJ
Telephone: 01273 911991
Website: www.presuming-ed.com
A redundant bank building upcycled into a coffeehouse filled with 80s gaming nostalgia, a 12-seater micro cinema in the original vault and a secret mezzanine beer garden.

Real Patisserie

Website: www.realpatisserie.co.uk
Independently run and self-sufficient shops making high quality artisan bread, and sweet and savoury food.

Real Pâtisserie

Church Road
147 Church Road
Hove BN3 2AE
Telephone: 01273 727 849

Real Pâtisserie

Kemp Town
34 St. George's Road
Kemp Town
Brighton BN2 1ED
Telephone: 01273 609 655

Real Pâtisserie

Open Market
Unit 2 Open Market
Marshalls Row
Brighton BN1 4JU
Telephone: 07475 792 657

Real Pâtisserie

Shoreham-By-Sea
4-6 East Street
Shoreham-By-Sea BN43 5ZE
Telephone: 01273 452 899

Real Pâtisserie

Trafalgar Street
43 Trafalgar Street
Brighton BN1 4ED
Telephone: 01273 691 551

Real Pâtisserie

Western Road
25 Western Road
Hove BN3 1AF
Telephone: 01273 711 110

Senor Buddha

9 Preston Rd
Brighton BN1 4QE
Telephone: 01273 567832
Website: www.senorbuddha.co.uk
Modern tapas and wine bar serving authentic Spanish tapas with a little East Asian twist.

Slake Spirits

Shoreham-by-Sea
West Sussex BN43 5HD
Telephone: 01273 457765
Website: www.slakespirits.com
Slake Spirits is an independent artisan gin distillery based in Shoreham-by-Sea, distilling fine artisan gin at the crossroads of science and nature.

Smorl's Houmous Falafel & Salad Bar
Unit 30, Brighton Open Market
Marshall's Row
Brighton BN1 4JU
Telephone: 01273 626315
Website: www.smorls.com
Independent market café specialising in their famous Smorl's Houmous, along with falafel, pitta pockets, salad boxes, meze cakes, soups and deli pots.

The Sussex Produce Company
88 High Street
Steyning
West Sussex BN44 3RD
Telephone: 01903 815 045
Website: www.thesussexproducecompany.co.uk
Award-winning food shop and café based in Steyning, West Sussex.

SussexFood
Bramber House
Refectory Road
University of Sussex
Falmer
East Sussex BN1 9QU
Telephone: 01273678221
Website: www.sussex.ac.uk/catering
Providing exceptional catering and conference services to students, staff and external visitors at the University of Sussex.

Veasey & Sons Fishmongers
17 Hartfield Road
Forest Row
East Sussex RH18 5DN
Telephone: 01342 822906
Website: www.veaseyandsons.co.uk
Fish the way it should be, fished the way it should be.

Vitality Hemp
Telephone: 07825 160141
Website: www.vitalityhemp.com
Hemp products made from hemp grown 100% naturally at the foot of the South Downs.

Wolfies Of Hove
90 Goldstone Villas
Hove BN3 3RU
Telephone: 01273 962395
Website: www.wolfieshove.co.uk
The best fish and chips in Brighton and Hove.

Wolfies Kitchen
98 Goldstone Villas
Hove BN3 3RU
Telephone: 07784 579573
Website: www.wolfies.kitchen
The best breakfast and brunch in Brighton and Hove.

INDEX

Other titles in the 'Get Stuck In' series

The Essex Cook Book features Daniel Clifford, The Anchor Riverside, Great Garnetts, Deersbrook Farm, Mayfield Bakery and lots more.
978-1-910863-25-1

The South London Cook Book features Jose Pizarro, Adam Byatt, The Alma, Piccalilli Caff, Canopy Beer, Inkspot Brewery and lots more.
978-1-910863-27-5

The Bristol Cook Book features Dean Edwards, Lido, Clifton Sausage, The Ox, and wines from Corks of Cotham plus lots more.
978-1-910863-14-5

The Oxfordshire Cook Book features Mike North of The Nut Tree Inn, Sudbury House, Jacobs Inn, The Muddy Duck and lots more.
978-1-910863-08-4

The Lancashire Cook Book features Andrew Nutter of Nutters Restaurant, Bertram's The Blue Mallard and lots more.
978-1-910863-09-1

The Liverpool Cook Book features Burnt Truffle, The Art School, Fraîche, Villaggio Cucina and many more.
978-1-910863-15-2

The Sheffield Cook Book - Second Helpings features Jameson's Tea Rooms, Craft & Dough, The Wortley Arms, The Holt, Grind Café and lots more.
978-1-910863-16-9

The Leeds Cook Book features The Boxtree, Crafthouse, Stockdales of Yorkshire and lots more.
978-1-910863-18-3

The Cotswolds Cook Book features David Everitt-Matthias of Champignon Sauvage, Prithvi, Chef's Dozen and lots more.
978-0-9928981-9-9

The Shropshire Cook Book features Chris Burt of The Peach Tree, Old Downton Lodge, Shrewsbury Market, CSons and lots more.
978-1-910863-32-9

The Norfolk Cook Book features Richard Bainbridge, Morston Hall, The Duck Inn and lots more.
978-1-910863-01-5

The Lincolnshire Cook Book features Colin McGurran of Winteringham Fields, TV chef Rachel Green, San Pietro and lots more.
978-1-910863-05-3

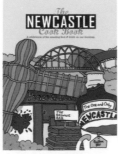

The Newcastle Cook Book features David Coulson of Peace & Loaf, Bealim House, Grainger Market, Quilliam Brothers and lots more.
978-1-910863-04-6

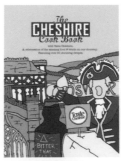

The Cheshire Cook Book features Simon Radley of The Chester Grosvenor, The Chef's Table, Great North Pie Co., Harthill Cookery School and lots more.
978-1-910863-07-7

The Leicestershire & Rutland Cook Book features Tim Hart of Hambleton Hall, John's House, Farndon Fields, Leicester Market, Walter Smith and lots more.
978-0-9928981-8-2

All books in this series are available from Waterstones, Amazon and independent bookshops.

FIND OUT MORE ABOUT US AT WWW.MEZEPUBLISHING.CO.UK